I0622427

Suddenly

A Widow's Story of
Unexpected Loss and Healing

Danell teNyenhuis Black

Copyright © 2024, Danell teNyenhuis Black

All rights reserved. No part of this book may be used or reproduced by any means, graphic, electronic, or mechanical (including any information storage retrieval system), without the express written permission from the author, except in the case of brief quotations for use in articles and reviews wherein appropriate attribution of the source is made.

Publishing support provided by
Ignite Press
5070 N. Sixth St. #189
Fresno, CA 93710
www.IgnitePress.us

ISBN: 979-8-9895900-0-1
ISBN: 979-8-9895900-1-8 (E-book)

For bulk purchases and for booking, contact:

Danell teNyenhuis Black
danellblackcounselor@gmail.com
https://danellblack.com/

Because of the dynamic nature of the internet, web addresses or links contained in this book may have been changed since publication and may no longer be valid. The content of this book and all expressed opinions are those of the author and do not reflect the publisher or the publishing team. The author is solely responsible for all content included herein.

Library of Congress Control Number: 2023922800

Cover design by Christopher Pana
Edited by Cathy Cruise
Interior design by Jetlaunch

FIRST EDITION

For Patrick

ACKNOWLEDGMENTS

I am so grateful to everyone who has been there for me since Patrick died. Thank you to those who reached out to me. No matter how brief the message, you will never know how much those texts and posts meant to me. I could have made an entire book of supportive messages, and I wish I had space to include all of them.

I want to give a special shout-out to the connections I made after Patrick died, including his high school classmates, patients, and coworkers. I haven't met many of you in person, but I've felt your support and enjoyed the memories you shared.

When you are widowed, you become part of a sisterhood that no one wants to join, but everyone is grateful for. Thank you to my sisters whom I have connected with over the years including Stacie del-Fierro Richard, Sonia Parso, Crystal Stupay, Laurie Smith, Patty Behrens, Janine Thompson Healy, Leicia Farrell Riding, Deanna Wright Ash, Lynne McNeil, Moon Ja, Jen Drake, Dorina Lazo Gilmore-Young, Heather Harrison, Roni Valle, Melissa Martinez, Trish Wright, Marcia Moore, Brianne Davis, and Nancy Saltzman. I may not see or connect with you often, but you've been there and know what it's like.

I am blessed to be part of several large, extremely close-knit families. The Hatch, Boyles, Prandini, and teNyenhuis families have always surrounded me with love. I can't imagine going through something like this without family to lean on.

Thank you to Sierra and Camille, my amazing, incredible, and loving daughters. Your resilience has amazed me, and I know your dad is as proud as I am of the women you have become. Thank you to my husband, Bruce, for being brave enough to join my large family! I came with a lot of baggage, and I know it's not easy marrying a widow. I am happy we found each other, and that I get to go through life with you. I love you!

Thank you to the teNyenhuis family: Barbara and Andre (Mom and Pop), Dan, Amy, Gabe, Jen, Dina, Jeff, Matt, Tina, and all my wonderful nieces and nephews! I have read about other widows who lost connection with their in-laws, and I am glad that was never a possibility.

Thank you to my family: Mom, Donald, Dad, Kandra, Denise, Scott, Dawan, Tom, Denny, Maudi, and all my remarkable nieces and nephews! I am blessed to always have 100 percent support from my parents, siblings, and their spouses. I wish Patrick could have met everyone who joined our family after we lost him. I know he would love you all!

Thank you to everyone who read or provided feedback on my book, including Sierra, Camille, Bruce, Dennis Boyles (Dad), Kandra Norsigian, Elizabeth Diane Tacchino (Mom), Denise Mohler, Dawan Utecht, Denny Boyles, Cathy Lamb, Nick Romano, Diana Durham, Lisa Bell, Roxy Ochoa, Ron Ballecer, and Stephanie Negin. A special thank you to my colleagues who read my book from a counseling perspective: Enedina Robles, LCSW; Katrina Blair, LMFT; Rosa Lomeli, LMFT; Gardenia Valencia, LCSW; Jessica Bloom, LMFT; Brenda Zarate, LMFT; and David Miller, LPCC, LMFT.

A huge thank you to my content editor, Lynn Thompson. I am eternally grateful to have been introduced to you, and it was a joy having your help turning my blog entries into a book. I couldn't have done it without you! If you need a great editor, you can reach Lynn at livingonpurposelynn@gmail.com.

Finally, a thank you to Everett O'Keefe at Ignite Press. Everett graduated from Hoover High School with Patrick and became my Facebook friend. I later found out that his business partner was John Riding, the late husband of Leicia Farrell-Riding, whom I met in my Gals In Growth widow group. One day, when I visited my mom and my stepfather, Donald Tacchino, they showed me a book written by one of Donald's former elementary students, Everett O'Keefe. I borrowed the book, *The Power of the Published*, and decided that I was meant to work with Everett to publish this book. Everett calls that providence, and I agree.

TABLE OF CONTENTS

PROLOGUE

Imagine you are taking a walk. The weather is perfect and the scenery is beautiful. As you walk, you hold the hand of the person you most want to walk this path with. There are hills, and sometimes you stumble, but your partner is always there to help you. You carry many memories with you. In the distance you can see many places you want to go. You anticipate these experiences with excitement. You have the path memorized and know exactly how to get there from here.

Suddenly, there is an earthquake worse than you ever imagined. A vast chasm opens up in the path in front of you. You feel your partner slipping, and then, they have disappeared. The destruction is so great that you can no longer see your future path. The experiences you had dreamed of are no longer possible.

At first you feel like jumping into the chasm and looking for your lost dreams. You don't see any other option. Moving forward alone is unthinkable. But you see another path leading away from the chasm.

This path is overgrown and is not as easy to navigate. Sometimes you need help clearing the way. Parts of the path seem dangerous and frightening, and the chasm always seems to be nearby.

As you make your way, you notice some interesting things ahead. Other people are traveling the path, and you begin to enjoy their company. They help clear the path and point out destinations you didn't realize were there. This route leads to a much different destination than you had planned. You haven't forgotten about your missing partner or your plans with them. You realize they would be happy that you found this new path and would want you to continue.

I wrote these words on the first anniversary of my husband Patrick's death. I am now on a completely different path I did not choose, but it is not as awful or scary as I'd thought. There have been new dreams and hopes for the future. Patrick walks this path with me and helps steer me in the right direction. He can no longer hold my hand, but keeps me from falling.

PART ONE

THE WORST DAY OF MY LIFE

ENTRY 1

APRIL 20, 2016

I wake up to a silent house. The clock says 6:45 a.m. I wonder where Patrick is. My husband, Patrick, is very dedicated to working out. When he received his master's in physical therapy, he gave the graduation speech, and it was about the importance of staying physically fit. Patrick does some type of workout almost every day of the week; some days, he does more than one. On weekday mornings he runs, lifts weights in the garage or rides his bike out Shaw Avenue to Quail Lakes, does a lap or two, and then returns home. He always tells me he doesn't particularly love working out, but does it anyway. I would love to have that kind of dedication!

I am not much of a morning person, so I usually sleep through his entire workout. Patrick sets his alarm for 5:30 a.m. and is generally finished by 6:45 a.m. Sometimes I wake up briefly when his alarm goes off, but I'm pretty good at sleeping through it, and I did that today.

It's odd that he's not home yet, but I have a conference call at seven, and I need to get moving if I want to be ready. I quickly change into what I jokingly call my day pajamas: capri-length black sweatpants with a stripe down the side, a sports bra, and a T-shirt. I run into the loft, turn my computer on, and then ask my 17-year-old daughter, Camille, to check the garage to see if her dad's bike is there. And then I dial into my call.

I love working from home. I've worked at Aetna for over 21 years and work with some of my closest friends. I began working at home a year ago, and although I miss the social interaction, I get much more done at home. I'm a plan sponsor liaison. I work with our sales and marketing team and a few national account customers. My 7:00 a.m. call is with a demanding customer, and I can't be distracted. I hope Patrick gets home soon.

Camille goes downstairs and returns a few minutes later to tell me Patrick's bike is gone. Ugh. He is very proud of his old, beat-up bike. He bought it in the mid-to-late '90s. I call his phone, but it rings with no answer. I must get off my call and rescue him from a flat tire. I worry that my customer or the sales team will be annoyed. I would ask Camille to go find him, but she needs to get to school on time.

At 7:10 a.m., I decide I can't wait any longer. I send an IM to my account manager to tell her I have a family emergency and need to step away. I'm unsure if a flat bike tire is an emergency, but I don't want Patrick to be late, since his patients are waiting for him.

I get in my car, which luckily already has the bike rack mounted, and head out to his usual route. I imagine him walking along the side of the road. I doubt he has his phone. He's invincible. Why would he need to carry his phone or any identification? I'm going to scold him when I see him.

ENTRY 2

PATRICK

Patrick bought his bike early in our marriage. The bike is ancient, and he considers himself an anti-cyclist, refusing to wear the usual cycling gear. I have a road bike and always extol the virtues of cycling and the benefits of getting a fancier bike, but he won't do it. He makes fun of the cycling outfits the serious cyclists wear and prides himself on wearing the most beat-up clothes he owns when riding. Patrick has a cyclist's body, and I like to imagine how great he would look in cycling shorts with a tight jersey, but he refuses.

On one of the few occasions when he did a ride with me and some of my cyclist friends, I could only imagine what they thought when he pulled up on that beater bike. I imagined their surprise when he kept up with them and climbed a hill as if on a lightweight road cycle.

He carries a saddle bag with tools and can usually repair a flat, but who knows what kind of mechanical trouble the bike might have?

ENTRY 3

THE SEARCH

I know the main route Patrick would have taken. He might have taken a couple of ways to get to the main road, Shaw Avenue. So I guess, and choose Locan Avenue. I don't see him there or when I get to Shaw, so I head east and scan the side of the road for a man walking a bike. A fire truck passes me, going in the opposite direction with its lights off. I'm a little alarmed to see it, although I think it wouldn't be driving away if there's an emergency.

We live in Clovis, California, a constantly growing suburb of Fresno. New housing developments are constantly popping up, and one or two roads are closed on any given day. I see the usual flashing signs ahead and assume the road is closed due to the new development on the street's south side. A small truck is parked there, and someone is beside it. I should investigate.

I pull over, get out, and walk over to the person I now see is a community service officer. I ask her what happened, and she says, "There was an accident." I tell her my husband was riding his bicycle and ask if I can see if he is there. She tells me the crash involved a motorcycle. She even adds the sound effect "vroom, vroom" to reassure me. She doesn't let me pass.

I return to my car and decide to investigate more, so I drive past Shaw, trying to think of a way to get closer. Patrick has CPR and first aid certification, and I know he would stop to help. Suddenly,

I realize this is too big of a coincidence. Patrick isn't home, he hasn't contacted me, *and* there was an accident. I've tried to stay calm and assume he's okay. Now I start to realize that something is probably wrong. And, if he *was* in an accident, I probably shouldn't go there. An inner voice tells me I need to go home to our daughter.

ENTRY 4

MEETING PATRICK

I remember the first time I saw Patrick. In June 1986 I was working as a typist for his cousin, John Prandini, in his physical therapy office, which was inside a local fitness club, Fresno Racquet Time. John was the brother of one of my high school track and cross-country coaches, Carlo Prandini. I knew one of their cousins was coming to work as a physical therapy aide for the summer, but I thought he would be older. In the front lobby, I saw a guy walking in. He was tall and dressed in a very '80s style, with light yellow pants, a T-shirt, and suspenders with palm trees. He was hot!

I later figured out I had seen Patrick before. Although we went to different high schools, we both ran track and cross-country. We would have been at the same meets many times during our high school years. I once went on a date with one of Patrick's best friends, John Wright, and Patrick was with him when we met. Although I often wonder why we couldn't have met sooner, I know we met when we were supposed to. We weren't instantly an item, but by the end of that summer, we had begun our 30-year love story.

I have always thought his last name (teNyenhuis) was cool! His father, Andre, is from the Netherlands. The lowercase te and capital N are the correct way to write it. To help people pronounce it, we always say T-9-house.

Me and Patrick, in 1986

ENTRY 5

DRIVING HOME

As I drive, I call my nephew, Nicholas Campbell, a police officer in our city. He tells me he isn't working, but agrees to try and get information. A few minutes later, he calls back to ask me to describe Patrick's bike. He mentions there has been an accident, and the rider did not have ID. I tell him his uncle refuses to wear the Road iD I had made for him. As a cyclist I have been taught the importance of always carrying ID when cycling in case you are unconscious after a crash. I have tried to get Patrick to wear his ID, but he was never worried about it.

I'm strangely calm. Maybe Patrick is knocked out and can't communicate. Probably everything is okay. Camille will be leaving for school, and I need to get home before she does, just in case. Walking into the house, I get a breaking news text reading, "Fatal bicycle vs. vehicle accident closes Shaw." And I know. I know I am a little obsessed with breaking news, and I tell myself this is what happens when you follow the news too closely. I have just received notification of death by a news alert. My brain refuses to process the information.

ENTRY 6

GRANDMA JANELL

When I was six years old, I experienced grief for the first time when my grandmother, Janell Hatch, died. Grandma Janell was my mother's stepmother; she could never have children, so she doted on my grandpa's children and grandchildren. Mom had a complicated relationship with her mother, and she always called Grandma Janell "Mom." My parents started all of their children's names with the letter D. They named me after my grandma, dropping the J and adding a D, so I always felt we had a special connection. Grandma Janell dressed nicely, loved spending time with her grandchildren, and always had clove chewing gum in her purse.

I remember going to her funeral and seeing her in the casket. She didn't look like she normally did, but her makeup was applied with care, and her hair looked perfect, so she was easily identifiable.

I also remember the flowers. Grandma was well-loved, and many people had sent arrangements. Now, whenever I smell many flowers, I think of my grandma's funeral.

Going to Grandma's funeral was not traumatic for me. I think it normalized death. I was sad, but I knew she had been in pain and I was glad she was no longer suffering. Death was no longer a mystery.

Several years after my grandma died, I had my first tragic experience. And, it was completely unexpected.

ENTRY 7

WHAT NOW?

I find Camille waiting in the living room when I walk in. I tell her there has been an accident, but I don't have any information. I explain her cousin is checking into it. Tears are rolling down my cheeks and I wipe them away, trying to hide my concern. We sit on the loveseat together, wondering what to do. Camille, so much like her dad, is a rock. She doesn't appear to be falling apart, and I try to hold it together for her.

I text my boss, Janet Spear.

> Wed, Apr 20, 7:53 AM
>
> Me: I have an emergency. My husband is missing and I think he might have been in an accident. I am waiting to hear. I will let you know.
>
> Janet: Oh my, okay. Hope all okay.
>
> Me: Please pray. I don't think it's ok but I'm still hoping.
>
> Janet: I am praying as well.

At 8:05 a.m., Nick calls me back to ask for more information. I send him a picture of Patrick's bicycle for the police. The only picture I have is one I took a few months ago. Patrick had gone for a bike ride, and a toothbrush was lodged in his spokes when he returned home. We thought it was hilarious, and I posted the picture on Facebook. Little did I know that I would later use the image to identify his bike.

After a short time, I realize I probably need to call people. I figured my nephew had told his mom—my sister, Denise—and I wonder why she hasn't called. Then I remember Nick takes after his dad and probably doesn't realize or care to activate the phone chain. I text Denise, and then she calls me. We talk on and off until we decide she should leave to pick up my older daughter, Sierra, who is 19 and at school in Long Beach, some 250 miles away. Denise also lives in the Los Angeles area, but is an hour and a half away from Sierra. We agree that Denise will call Sierra and tell her she needs to come get her to bring her home, and that she needs to pack a bag. I worry that she will panic, but I don't want to tell her the news when she is alone. I pray that Denise will not hit traffic and will get there as quickly as possible. And I know, without even asking, she will alert the rest of our family. It's just what we do, and she is the best at it.

8:18 a.m. – Texted my friends Lisa Walthall and Shelly Cruce at work.

Wed, Apr, 20, 8:21 AM

Me: Hi friends. There was a fatal bike accident on Shaw and Patrick is missing. My nephew is trying to get details. Please pray.

Lisa: Of course we're praying!!

Shelly: Let us know

Notifying Patrick's family is a little different. His parents, Barbara and Andre, also known as Mom and Pop, live across town, and I don't want to give them news like this over the phone. His oldest brother, Daniel, lives in Nebraska. His younger brother, Gabriel, lives nearby, but he is at the high school teaching the class Camille would have been in if she was in school. His sister, Dina, is running errands and planning to come to my house when she finishes. I don't want to call her either. The youngest, Matthew, also a physical therapist and a physical therapy manager at a large hospital, is at work, so I call him. He calls me back, and we talk briefly. Matt stays calm, which I appreciate, since I am having trouble holding it together. I want to stay strong for everyone.

ENTRY 8

THE LATE BUS

My family lived in a large two-story house for four years, beginning when I was eight. Our home was located in what we called "the country," which meant it was miles and miles from town. Actually, it was only four miles from city hall, but it always seemed much further.

Our house was on the corner of Shaw and Dewolf, which, at the time, were both two-lane roads. Shaw was, and is, one of the main thoroughfares connecting our city, Clovis, California, to Fresno, California.

Our home was on two-and-a-half acres, bordered by two roads and an almond orchard. Our property consisted of a house with four bedrooms, one bathroom, a kitchen, a dining room, a living room, and a den. We had two separate garages and a large barn. In the front of the house was a small corral, and on the side was a more extensive pasture that was also a tiny almond orchard.

Over the years, we had cows, a horse, pigs, chickens, geese, rabbits, and probably other animals I'm forgetting. We also had an assortment of dogs, including a large Saint Bernard named Morley. I was the third of four children, and we had a blast living in that house!

Since the house was so far from town, we took a bus to and from school. In fifth grade, I ran track and cross-country, and I would ride the late bus home. The late bus had a longer route, and our house was one of the last stops. Depending on the time of year, the sun might be setting as I arrived home.

The bus would travel on the west side of Shaw and park across the street from my house, which meant the bus driver would get out and use her stop sign for me to cross the street.

One evening, when I was ten, I was riding the late bus home after practice. As the bus slowed to a stop near my house, I saw my brother and sister jogging along the road by the orchard. My eyes barely registered piles of clothing in the orchard's second row. I noticed them because they didn't belong, but I was more focused on my siblings. They didn't normally go jogging, so I was surprised to see them. Then I remembered that, since my sister played high school softball, she was trying to stay in shape between seasons.

After the bus stopped, my bus driver, Irene, walked me across the road and returned to the bus. My siblings were still 20 feet or so away from me. I noticed a car parked on the side of the road and was startled to see a strange man approaching my six-year-old brother, Denny. The man turned to Denise, who was 16, and asked if our parents were home. His face was white, and he was trembling. He said he had hit two men.

I'm not sure who went in to get my parents, but I think it was me. They quickly called an ambulance. I guess I looked in the orchard again and realized the piles of clothing were actually people who were not moving.

My brother and sister had also identified the objects as clothing. My sister thought trash was flying out of someone's truck. I can't imagine how much worse it would have been for them if they had known what they were seeing.

My sister Dawan was 14 at the time. She remembers walking out to the road afterward as the police and ambulance were arriving. An older girl approached her and asked if she had seen her father and uncle. She told Dawan they had come to check on a dog she had hit while pulling a horse trailer. Our dogs were in the orchard, and in all the commotion we hadn't noticed that Morley was lying down, which was unusual.

My sister realized the girl's father and uncle were the victims, and she took her over to talk to the police.

The paramedics told my mother that the men had multiple bones broken in their bodies. Both men died instantly. The man driving the car was driving west when the sun was setting, and he didn't see them.

My parents took Morley to the vet, and he didn't return home.

My mom remembers having prior contact with the family when our steer got out and went to their house. They lived a few houses away and across the road from our house. We'll never know why they didn't just call or park on our side of the road. I remember that the men's wives came to our house to talk to us at some point later. I think it provided a bit of closure for all of us.

I've never forgotten that girl, and I wonder how her life turned out after enduring such an awful tragedy. I hope she was able to find peace and resilience. She was around the same age as my daughters are now, who, 40 years later, have potentially lost their father too, only half a mile east on the same road.

ENTRY 9

OUR LITTLE BROTHERS

When I met Patrick, his youngest brother, Matt, was only 10 years old, and I think of him as my little brother. He is a lot like his brother and very calm under pressure. I know I can count on him. After texting and calling a few times, we agree he should leave work and head to my house.

8:28 a.m. – Realizing Patrick's absence is alarming enough that my best friend, Cathy Lamb, will forgive me for bothering her at work, I text her. I am beginning to lose it a bit at this point and can only give short explanations.

> Wed, Apr 20, 8:38 AM
>
> Me: My husband has not come home from his bike ride.
>
> Cathy: Crud! What can I do?
>
> Me: Nothing. It's a waiting game. I know there was an accident.
>
> Cathy: How do you know?
>
> Me: Went there. News. Nephew. Fatal.

Right after texting Cathy, I call Patrick's office, San Joaquin Valley Rehabilitation (SJVR) Clovis, and speak to the office manager, Jennifer. I can barely talk, so she agrees to contact Kevin, Patrick's boss.

Kevin calls back a few minutes later, and I agree to keep him updated. Then Cathy calls and tells me she is coming over.

In the meantime, my little brother, Denny, shows up with three of his four children. They help me tidy up my house. I know it is about to be filled with people, and I am bothered by the clutter. Camille is still calm, but looks ashen, and I am glad her cousins are here now.

I was blessed to grow up in a large family, and Patrick also came from a large family. My children have seven sets of aunts and uncles and over 20 first cousins, including some from blended families. I am more grateful than ever for the family today. I know I am not alone.

ENTRY 10

THE WAITING CONTINUES

As we wait, I continue to reach out to friends and family.

8:46 a.m. – Text to Dina, Patrick's sister. She lives in Shaver, about an hour away from Clovis. She had planned to stop by this morning to pick something up, so I know she's already in town.

> Wed, Apr 20, 8:46 AM
>
> Me: Are you in town yet? If possible come straight here.
>
> Dina: I'm at Sam's club
>
> Me: Ok you are coming here right?
>
> Dina: Yes I was planning on after 10 if that's still ok.
>
> Me: Yes. Something happened.
>
> Dina: Are you ok? I can come by after I leave here.
>
> Me: Yeah. Just come here.

Wed, Apr 20, 9:00 AM

Matt: I am heading to your house.

Me: Still no news.

Me: Ok

Me: Should you just get your parents?

Matt: I was thinking about that. Let me think about it. I will let you know.

Me: Ok. I think maybe you should.

Matt: Ok.

9:02 a.m. – I call my sister-in-law, Jen, to contact Patrick's brother, Gabe. As I mentioned, he is a teacher at the high school, and Jen will know the quickest way to reach him. She tells me she is in Phoenix to pick up my niece, Caitlin, who is moving back to Clovis. She agrees to contact the school.

9:19 a.m. – Nick calls to check in, and I tell him Denny is at my house.

9:40 a.m. – Text from my cousin, Wendy, in Oregon. She is the daughter of my mom's sister, Joni.

Wed, Apr 20, 9:40 AM

Wendy: Is everything ok?

Me: I don't think so

Wendy: Your mom called my mom hysterical and she couldn't understand her.

9:42 a.m. – Call to Aunt Joni – three minutes

9:46 a.m. – Call from Kevin at SJVR – three minutes

9:57 a.m. – Message from Dyia Kwalwasser, a good friend and the mother of Camille's close friend, Peyton

> Wed, Apr 20 9:57 AM
>
> Dyia: I'm not sure what's going on. I'm getting lots of texts from Peyton that there might have been an accident this morning. Let me know if you need anything!!!! I'm here for you guys.
>
> Me: Thanks. We don't have official word.
>
> Me: But I'm pretty sure it's Patrick. He refuses to carry ID with him so that's making it hard.
>
> Dyia: Oh my gosh! Is Camille with you?
>
> Me: Yes. And lots of family.
>
> Me: My sister is going to get Sierra.
>
> Dyia: Ok, I'm off the rest of the day. Whatever you need don't hesitate to ask!! I'm so sorry. There are no words.
>
> Me: I just want official confirmation.
>
> Me: Thanks

10:06 a.m. – Text from Misty Hessling, one of my close friends at work.

> Wed, Apr 20, 10:06 AM
>
> Misty: No need to respond. I know you are over-whelmed and in shock but please give yourself a hug from me. Sorry doesn't even cover it. I can only imagine what you are going thru. I won't bombard you with one more person stopping by but if you want company, whatever, please let me know. I wish I could fix this for you.

10:16 a.m. – Text from Linda Crews, good friend and mother of one of Camille's close friends, Julia.

> Wed, Apr 20, 10:16 AM
>
> Linda: There are no words. If there's anything I can do, don't hesitate to say.
>
> Me: Thank you
>
> Linda: I'm at school with all of the girls with the psychologist.
>
> Me: Oh good

10:17 a.m. – Call from my sister, Dawan, and brother-in-law, Tom. They are in Europe on a business trip for Tom. We are all extremely close; I can tell they want to be home.

10:58 a.m. – Text from Cherie Kirk, a good friend and the mother of Camille's friend, Mikaela.

Wed, Apr 20, 10:58 AM

Cherie: Praying for you and your family

Me: Thank you

Cherie: Mikaela said Camille likes spaghetti, can I bring some today or sometime soon? We just want to help in any way we can. When my dad passed it was nice not having to think about dinner.

Me: Sure

Denise calls to let me know my dad and stepmother are on their way from their home in Arroyo Grande, two-and-a-half hours from my home. I need my dad; I'm glad he is on the way. I walk outside for some air and see my brother-in-law, Wes, walking up. I lived with Wes and Denise a few times during college when they were married. He cosigned for my first car and has been like my second father. I hadn't even thought about him being there, but suddenly, I'm overwhelmed with emotion and sob in his arms. When you're experiencing grief and shock, you don't even know who you need, and when they show up before you think about it, you are so grateful.

ENTRY 11

PUT A RING ON IT

Patrick and I discussed marriage early in our relationship, and we always knew that it wouldn't happen until after we had both finished school, which would be six years after we met.

Patrick had three years left at the University of the Pacific, and I had four years left at Fresno State. After he graduated, he began attending the Chapman College at Children's Hospital physical therapy program in Los Angeles.

We had a long-distance relationship for most of that time, making the wait seem longer. When I was close to finishing college, and Patrick had two years left, I thought he would ask me to marry him soon.

Around that time, we went out for a nice dinner to celebrate Valentine's Day. He gave me a wrapped gift, and when I opened it, I found a package of plastic dress-up rings for kids. He had taken one out and replaced it with a small diamond promise ring. I loved my promise ring and thought the gift was very creative. I couldn't wait to see what he had planned for the proposal!

We were at his parents' house for Christmas that year, and he took me into a room to give me my gift. I was excited when he handed me a ring box, but puzzled that it looked worn. And why wasn't he on one knee? I opened the box, and there it was! A guitar pick!? He had bought me a guitar. I think his mother scolded him when I told her how he had given it to me. He acted innocent, but I believe he was teasing me.

Next up was Valentine's Day, 1991. He bought me a lovely outfit, but no ring. I wanted to plan the wedding I knew would take place in the summer of 1992, but I needed to be engaged first! I was getting impatient!

Around this time, Patrick started telling me he couldn't afford a ring. He wanted me to give him my promise ring back, and he would use it to propose.

I told him that was unnecessary. By then, I was working full-time as a teacher and could qualify to buy a ring. He didn't like that plan.

So I waited, and it became a frequent semi-argument. Patrick would tease me about being materialistic. And maybe I was, but I wanted that symbol of our engagement. It seems silly when I think about it now, but it was important to me.

The next time he visited, I restarted the discussion, and he tried to get me to give him the promise ring again. When I mentioned that I could buy the ring, he sighed.

"Oh, whatever, the ring is in my backpack," he said. I went and dug it out and started dancing around and calling my family. He loved to tease me about that, but I know he always knew how much I loved him. He eventually asked me to marry him before I put it on, but he always said my greed ruined his romantic proposal! And my response was always, "Whatever!"

Patrick and me in the early years

Our engagement photo

ENTRY 12

CONFIRMATION

As we wait for news, family and friends continue arriving. My mom comes shortly after Denny. Matt brings Mom and Pop. Dina and Gabe arrive separately. I am vaguely aware that Denny is on the phone talking about the accident, and I hear him talk about identification. I don't ask questions because I don't want to rush the inevitable. Denny tells me Patrick's cousin, Carlo Prandini, is going to the accident scene. He is the school district's deputy superintendent, and the police notified him, since the accident was by Clovis East High School. As I mentioned, Carlo was one of my high school track and cross-country coaches and is the reason I met Patrick.

Denny explains that the police will not let my nephew go to the scene to identify Patrick, so Carlo will identify him.

A short time later, I hear that Carlo is coming to my house, and I walk outside to wait. Carlo arrives with Barry Jager, an associate superintendent. Barry is a close friend of Gabe teNyenhuis, and Patrick ran a marathon with them. They walk up, and I barely register Carlo telling me about Patrick. I thought I was prepared, then he hands me a baggie with Patrick's watch and wedding band, and suddenly it is *real*. I just walk away to find Camille and gather Patrick's family. I slip Patrick's ring on my finger and hand Camille his watch.

A chaplain is with Carlo and Barry, and he answers questions to the best of his ability. He asks if we would like to pray, and we all agree. He tells us that there is some suspicion that the driver was impaired. After he leaves, I talk to Gabe, Dina, Matt, Mom, and Pop. I tell them that Patrick did not like funerals and probably wanted to be cremated or buried in a cardboard box, but I can't imagine that. We all agree that the funeral is for us and that he would forgive us. I have always thought that the greatest gift he ever gave me was his family (and I'm just going to include my girls as part of that gift). This gift has never been more evident than it is during this whole difficult, awful process. I don't know how people deal with tragedy and grief without family. I am blessed to have two huge families to surround me with love.

11:12 a.m. – Cathy calls Patrick's boss, Kevin, to notify him.

ENTRY 13

NOTIFYING SIERRA

Denise calls and tells me she has reached Sierra's apartment. Sierra answers the door and takes Denise into her room. Denise hands her the phone.

"Hi, sweetheart," I say.

"Mom, what's happening?" Sierra answers.

"Your dad was in an accident."

"Is he okay?" Sierra asks.

I pause. "I'm sorry, Sierra, he didn't make it."

"What? Noooo, nooooo, whyyyy?" She sobs.

My heart breaks. I question whether telling her over the phone is the best decision, but she will be in the car for four hours, and she would have known something was wrong. I know that would be worse. I'm surprised she didn't call me while waiting for Denise to get there. I'm grateful that Camille and I had time to absorb it slowly, and we were together the whole time. It was sudden and shocking for Sierra, and I know her cries will be forever etched in my memory. I just want to wrap my arms around her and love on her. I am so grateful that Denise is there to get her for me. I'm sure it is also the most challenging thing she has ever done. I tell Sierra I love her and will see her soon, and then I hang up so they can get on the road. As they drive home, Sierra talks and texts with Camille and her friends. I check in a few times too.

11:24 a.m. – Text from my dear friend and adopted cousin, Dawn Kuhl. Her husband, Mike, was the bass player for Patrick's Bluegrass band, Steam Donkeys.

> Wed, Apr 20, 11:24 AM
>
> Dawn: Oh my darling. My heart is breaking. I love you. What can I do to help you right now?
>
> Me: Thank you. I have lots of support but feel free to come by if you want.

11:26 a.m. – Text from Dawn Vizzolini, a good friend and the mother of Camille's close friend, Logan.

> Wed, Apr 20 11:26 AM
>
> Dawn: I just wanted to let you know we're here if you need anything. Please don't hesitate. I don't want to burden you as I know there's so much going on but please know we love you all and we will be here, always, for whatever you need. Plz give the girls a hug and love for us. We love u all. We will be praying.
>
> Me: Thank you. Maybe Logan can come see Camille after school.
>
> Dawn: She wants to. She just asked if she could be with her now but she didn't want to be in anybody's way.
>
> Me: Absolutely she can come now.
>
> Dawn: But if she wants her to be with her she would love to be. Are u home?
>
> Me: Yes
>
> Dawn: Ok, on way

11:28 a.m. – Text from Erin Haagenson, the mother of one of Sierra's closest friends, Olivia.

> Wed, Apr 20, 11:28 AM
>
> Erin: Danell, I'm so sorry this is horrible and unfair. Anything I can do I'm here.
>
> Me: Thank you. Maybe Liv can come when Sierra gets here?
>
> Erin: Yes I will bring her. Can I bring you anything?
>
> Me: No, I have lots of family here.
>
> Erin: Okay that's good, I'm here for you anytime in the future.

11:30 a.m. – Text from Olivia Haagenson, Sierra's good friend since second grade, and her college roommate. Olivia was unfortunately home from school due to an accident, and I was glad that meant she would be there when Sierra got home.

> Wed, Apr 20, 11:30 AM
>
> Olivia: I'm so sorry Danell. This is devastating and I'm heartbroken. You and Patrick were second parents to me and I don't even know what to say. My mom and I are here for your whole family and will do anything you need.
>
> Me: Thank you. See you soon

11:30 a.m. – Message from Crystal Stupay, a friend and former coworker at Aetna who lost her husband suddenly, two years before Patrick died.

Wed, Apr 20, 11:30 AM

Crystal: Danell, Kelli just called and gave me the news. My heart is breaking for you. I know this journey, this club known as widows nobody ever wants to join, all to well. Nothing anybody is going to say is going to make you feel better honey. Some people don't know what to say, I still get that to this day and it's been almost 2 years for me. I'm sure you're probably still in shock right now I know I was for at least a year. I can totally understand.

Me: Thank you so much Crystal, that means a lot. I'm sure I will call.

Crystal: It's something I will never get over, just learn to live with. You are lucky that you have such a supportive large family. Sending hugs your way. Please let me know if there's anything I can do. As well as when the services are.

Me: Ok. Thank you.

11:42 a.m. – Linda Crews sends me a picture of Camille's friends at school, meeting with the school psychologist and sending Camille love. Two girls, Logan and Tess, attend different high schools, and I am surprised that they all made the effort to be together. I let Linda know that they are all welcome to visit Camille and she assures me she will send them over.

Camille has been by my side all morning, leaning on my shoulder. When I stepped away, Cathy took my place; at one point, Camille was resting her head on Nick's shoulder. I have been concerned about her, so I am relieved when her friends arrive a short time later, and they all head upstairs into her room. I'm surprised they all fit in there, and I'm so grateful that she has her tribe with her. Before long, I hear laughter, and I can relax a little.

Over the next several hours, I receive messages from friends and family. The outpouring of support touches me.

After what seems like forever, Denise and Sierra arrive. A large contingent of friends and relatives is waiting for them, including all of Sierra's close friends from high school. But first, Camille and I run outside, and the three of us hug and cry. I look at the watch on Camille's wrist, take Patrick's ring off, and hand it to Sierra. I can tell she is happy to have something of her father's.

ENTRY 14

THE FIRST OF MANY HIDDEN TREASURES

For Christmas in 2015, I bought Patrick a small laptop with a video camera. Before that, we had just shared computers, and I thought it was time he had his own. Patrick pretended that he didn't like technology, but liked to borrow ours! He had begun recording himself playing his banjo, and I knew that in the week between his birthday and death, I had heard him playing Paul McCartney songs.

As we sit around in shock and disbelief, I pull out his laptop and find a treasure trove of recordings. The best is a recording of him playing "Blackbird." As I sit there and listen to the lyrics, "Take these broken wings and learn to fly," I feel like I'm listening to a love letter from Patrick.

The local news media has been in contact with us. Denny is a former newspaper reporter, so he is the media contact. I agree to speak to a news reporter off the air. I only agree because the reporter, Gene Haagenson, is the grandfather of Sierra's friend, Olivia, and I know him personally. I share the video with him; he includes it in his story. I'm glad that I can share a bit of Patrick. I upload the video to his YouTube channel, Patrickt9.

I continue to receive a steady stream of condolences the rest of the day and into the night. After everyone leaves, Denise, the girls, and I go to bed.

Denise will stay with us for the time being. Camille takes our dog, Aggie, to bed with her, Sierra climbs into bed with me, and Denise takes Sierra's bed. I try to go to sleep, and I just can't. When I hear Sierra sleeping, I tiptoe out of my room and crawl into bed with my big sissy. She holds me while I sob.

PART TWO

THE AFTERMATH

ENTRY 15

F or the rest of the day and many days to follow, family and friends surround us and give us love. I often walk into my bedroom and look longingly at the bed. I want to collapse into the fetal position and sob. But I know I can't. And I know I don't need to. I have more love for me in the house than I can imagine.

Most of all, I have Patrick's love. He would want me to be okay.

As Patrick's death replays in my head, my mind frequently returns to the agony of having Sierra four hours away when it happened. After Denise called her, Sierra did not ask any questions, and she did not call or text anyone, not even her sister. This is somewhat of a miracle, as Sierra usually texts me frequently. I believe Patrick was also watching over her so that she would not get the news until Denise was there.

On April 21, I do not leave the house. I sit in numb shock, waiting to figure out what to do next. As hard as the worst day of my life was, I have no idea that the following days will each be a different kind of hard.

When a family member dies, one of the first things you must do is decide on a funeral home if you have yet to make these arrangements. Patrick and I had talked about making a will, but we thought we would have plenty of time. Our main reason would have been to ensure the girls were cared for; we knew our families would handle that. Our lives were simple enough that it didn't cause issues not to have a will.

I have to decide on a funeral home right away. We are Catholic, so I choose Whitehurst, the funeral home that handled every Catholic funeral I have ever attended. You have to make an appointment to go to the funeral home, and because Patrick's body won't be immediately released by the coroner, the appointment isn't until Friday.

As we are sitting around in shock, my mother-in-law calls to let me know that her brother, Patrick's Zio (Uncle) Angelo, has died. He had been sick and she thinks Patrick's death might have been too much for him. We coordinate funerals, and plan their services one day apart.

Luckily, we are never alone. There is a common misconception that people don't want to be bothered when grieving. I now realize you should never assume anything when it comes to grief. Being there is one of the most important things you can do. When in doubt, just ask if they would mind company.

On Friday, April 22, 11 of us are seated around a table making funeral arrangements. I don't know how people would ever do that by themselves. Whenever there is a difficult decision, a family member helps me make it or agrees to take charge. For instance, someone helps decide on food for the memorial service, and others help design the memorial program.

By Friday night, Dawan and Tom return from Europe, and Patrick's brother, Dan, his wife, Amy, and the kids arrive from Nebraska, so we are finally together. Friends have started a meal train, and many people bring food, so we don't have to worry about cooking or shopping.

Also on Friday night, the detective, Drew Mosher, and the police chief, Matt Basgall (who happens to be a high school classmate of mine), come by to provide an update on the case. Drew and Matt tell us the driver was on call as an unofficial taxi for friends. He was coming off a meth high and possibly fell asleep at the wheel, drifted over, and hit Patrick. Patrick died instantly. There are a lot of questions and a lot of tears. We appreciate the update.

ENTRY 16

*"I never would have made it if I could not have laughed.
It lifted me momentarily out of this horrible situation,
just enough to make it livable."*
—Viktor Frankl

After Drew and Matt left, we were speechless, taking in all the new information, huddled on chairs and sofas in our living room. Then I remembered the thrift store contest we had a few weeks ago and asked the girls to recreate the presentation.

Patrick's dry sense of humor was legendary in our family. Sierra and Camille share their father's sense of humor, which has gotten us through many difficult times. One of our favorite things to do as a family was to visit thrift shops in San Luis Obispo, near the central coast of California.

Patrick liked to be a miser and usually bought his work clothes at thrift shops. I think his employees knew where he shopped without even being told. He also liked to find little treasures there, and the girls loved buying clothes. I usually bought books or odd household items.

A short time before Patrick died, he and the girls took a day trip to the beach, went thrifting, and decided to have a contest. They could each spend five dollars, and I had to judge whose item was the "Most Awesome."

The girls spent their $5 on clothing. Their presentations involved dramatically walking down the stairs wearing their purchases and working hard to sell them. Camille was first, and she came downstairs in this ridiculous white, gauzy pantsuit with military-style patches sewn on.

The outfit looked like a uniform created to be a Halloween costume. It was all white with a collar, elastic at the waist, and cuffed wrists and ankles. There were 30 to 40 patches including stars and wings.

Camille strutted down the stairs, then jumped off and pointed at the suit. As she later said, the outfit spoke for itself and didn't require words.

Sierra was next. Sierra has a speech, debate, and mock trial background and is very persuasive! She strutted down and twirled in the most ridiculous T-shirt I have ever seen. Sierra said she loved that someone made an effort to display their love of frogs by cutting out a panel in the T-shirt and carefully sewing in a piece of material with green frogs on lily pads and other frogs leaping over them. Then they decided it would be a little more awesome to keep that extra part of the T-shirt, cut it into a fringe, and add beads, which they hung over the frog panel. I was dying during her presentation!

Patrick had gone last and announced he knew his $5 find would be the most awesome. He bought an apple parer/corer/slicer. He gave an elaborate presentation on the virtues of this handy kitchen tool.

I don't eat many apples, but I could see the appeal of using the tool. I felt it was a good purchase, but Sierra was my hands-down winner. I'm not sure he ever forgave me for not choosing him!

After the encore presentation, the girls share other stories about their dad—exactly what we all need. We've been steeped in grief and need this break of laughter connected with Patrick memories. I have not heard this much laughter in our house since Wednesday, and it's a welcome change. Humor has always been a big part of our family, and I'm glad we can use it to lift our spirits.

We vow to continue the tradition; other family members plan to participate in the next contest. The Most Awesome $5 Find game will continue, and we will all remember the precious memories associated with it.

ENTRY 17

MISSING PIPES – APRIL 25, 2016

Patrick playing the banjo by the fire

My brother has a close friend named Phillip Weathers. A few weeks before Patrick died, we were all sitting around a fire pit at Denny's house. Patrick was playing his banjo and singing corny songs. Someone snapped a picture of him in his signature flannel and it became one of our most treasured photos after he died. He was also trying to convince Phillip and Denny to take up pipe smoking with him. Despite his dedication to health and wellness, Patrick took up pipe smoking in his forties. His father had smoked a pipe when he was young, and Patrick seemed to feel that being a pipe smoker put him in an exclusive club. He had such a great time with Phillip and Denny that night that he decided to order pipes for them. They were hilarious. Denny's was a corn cob pipe, and Phillip's was some ridiculously long thing. I knew they had arrived, but I could never find them. I thought they were sitting in boxes on a coffee table. As things started unfolding the day he died, I knew my house would be full of people, so of course, all I could think about was how messy it was. I think the boxes were thrown into recycling while people were helping me clean up.

While trying to verify that he did receive both pipes, I searched our purchase history. That was when I saw he had also ordered a unique lighter—a little golden man with an enormous appendage from which the flame would shoot out! Only Patrick would order something like this. And the shipment hadn't arrived yet! I told the girls we would be getting a package that would make us laugh. The box came on a Monday. I got the mail and left it on the table.

We had a private viewing appointment at the funeral home that day, so opening the mail was not a priority. That was a tough day for all of us.

Over the weekend, there had been much discussion and tears in deciding whether or not to see him. Everyone wanted to protect me, but I knew I had to see him. There was no way anyone was going to stop me. There are no words to describe seeing your dead husband when he has been ripped from your life so violently.

I was escorted into the room, but I don't remember who was with me. I know it was one or all of my siblings. My dad followed, and as I sank to the floor, he was suddenly there to hold me up. For some reason, I could only say, "I'm sorry, I'm sorry, I'm sorry." I was telling Patrick I was sorry that this happened to him, but

I know it also expressed my grief. He was on a table on top of a blanket, which was easier than seeing him in the casket.

His skin felt soft, yet cold. His wedding band had a scrape on it when Carlo returned it to me, so I had to check his hand. There was an injury, but it didn't look bad. He looked peaceful and didn't look like he had suffered too much. But it wasn't him. He had never looked like that in life. I knew he was gone. I have so many pictures of him; this is just one small memory.

On the way home, Denny was driving, and I started talking about the package. I realized that somehow Denny had not heard me talking about it! So I decided he could open it. Inside the package, there were actually *two* lighters! I'm not sure who Patrick bought these lighters for, but we all got a really good laugh out of them.

Denny later said opening the box was a "real mix of sadness, laughter, and love."

"It was such a Patrick thing," he said. "And I was sad that those moments were ending." Denny said he also felt laughter and love "at the ridiculousness of it." He noted, "If Patrick had lived, I would have brought that lighter every time I smoked a cigar with him because he would have completely expected me to." He added that he was also positive Patrick would have said, "Nice dick" every time.

The lighters were on the mantle for a while, "saluting" Patrick's picture. I finally hid them after one too many kids noticed them (oops)!

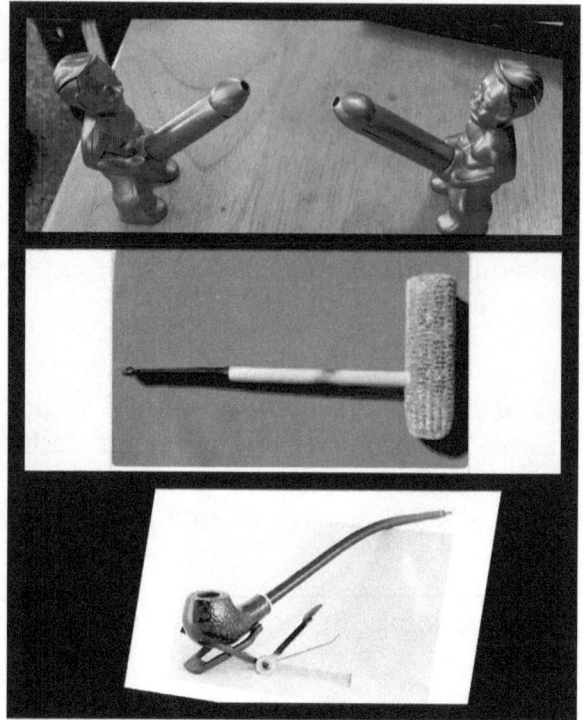

The pipes and lighters

We thought about what we would do with the lighters and decided to share them in the Cranberry Lambic tradition.

Patrick and his siblings all enjoy beer. Patrick had taken up the hobby of making beer and, although I am not a beer drinker, I've been told he made very good beer. Many years ago, someone (possibly Patrick's sister, Dina, or her husband, Jeff Young) bought a pack of beer called Cranberry Lambic. I never tasted it, but it is rumored to be the most foul-tasting beer ever! Once the first beer was drunk, the purchaser decided they couldn't finish the rest and would "gift" them to others. Over the years, the siblings devised elaborate schemes to sneak the beers to their unsuspecting victims. You might find one in your fridge after guests left. Or maybe it was in the ice chest you carried home after a party. One particularly cruel sibling carefully replaced the label with a Sierra Nevada one. The rule is, if you start drinking it, you have to finish!

When Patrick died, the siblings agreed it would be fitting to leave a bottle with him to ensure he was "it."

So, in keeping with the beer tradition, now these lighters are passed around and hidden in each other's houses.

I gave one to my niece, Alyssa, to hide in Denny's house and one to my niece, Caitlin, to hide in Gabe's house. Gabe found his quickly, but Denny's was in his 49er helmet, and after several months, we had to drop all kinds of hints. It was hilarious when he finally noticed it.

More recently, we had a gathering at Matt and Tina's house. Denny mentioned that a lighter might make an appearance. As I left Matt's house, I realized I hadn't heard if it was left there. Denny later told me he had carefully opened a bag of tortilla chips, placed the lighter inside, then resealed the bag and left it there. A few days later, my 19-year-old niece, Ella teNyenhuis, had friends over for tacos. And, of course, they found the lighter!

I'm not sure where the second lighter is these days, but I know that on Patrick's last birthday, one was hidden in someone's belongings as they left our house.

I'm so glad that Patrick's humor has outlasted him!

ENTRY 18

SAYING GOODBYE – APRIL 27, 2017

T he rosary and funeral turn out exactly like I imagined. I'm touched to see how many people attend, and I can feel how much love they all show us. At the same time, everything is a blur, and each day is hard to get through.

At the rosary, a physical therapist, George Drysdale, introduces himself, and we find out he was on the scene when Patrick died. He tells me he and his wife have been praying for the girls and me, and his wife wanted me to know she was sending her love.

The funeral is standing-room only. The sheer number of people here touches me. Before the service starts, I have time to greet a few people, which helps me relax. We've planned a full Catholic mass with music provided by bluegrass musicians, including Doug Bremseth, Patrick's banjo instructor. My cousin, Travis Holland, agreed to sing, and I am pleasantly surprised when his wife, Desiree, joins him. I've never heard her sing, and her beautiful voice lifts my spirits. Denny wrote a touching eulogy with help from other siblings, which is read by John Prandini.

After the funeral, the attendees linger in small groups. I really want to greet them all, but I also want to get through the whole day, so I usher the girls into the town car following the hearse, and we begin the funeral procession to the cemetery. There is a brief graveside service, and although there would typically be a receiving line afterward, I feel it is too much for the girls. I ask the

funeral director to conclude the service and make an announcement about the reception. We get into the car and return to the
church for the reception.

When we get there, we are finally able to relax. I can greet family members and friends and am excited to see a contingent of
Patrick's Phi Delta Theta fraternity brothers. There is a touching slideshow, which Jill Holstein and Mark Dorman lovingly put
together. The music includes some of Patrick's. During this slide
show, I see the Instagram posts Sierra and Camille had made the
day Patrick died. I hadn't seen them before, and I feel tears slide
down my cheeks as I recognize the love conveyed in them.

I am relieved and exhausted at the end of the day. I am hopeful
that the grief will get more manageable now.

ENTRY 19

LOVED AND RESPECTED – APRIL AND MAY 2016

In the following weeks, I found out from Patrick's boss and coworkers at the hospital how difficult it was for them to hear the news that he had died. Patrick was well-loved by his patients and staff and was an excellent physical therapist. After he died, I heard from many coworkers and patients, and they confirmed what I already knew from personal experience.

Many years earlier, Patrick sent me an email when I was just starting to experience back pain, which would eventually turn out to be hip pain and lead to my hip replacement. This period was challenging and frustrating for me, but he was with me every step of the way and this email says it all. He loved me so much and took such good care of me. He couldn't fix everything, but he would have if he could. God, I miss him.

> You just seemed so frustrated last night and this morning that I didn't even know what to say to you. Now that I've had some time to think about it, I know what I want to say:
>
> Your back WILL get better. It may take a while, but it will. If I have to see to it myself, it will. There is no way I will permit my wife to be thrown into the wastebasket of chronic pain. It will not happen.

This is my promise to you. You can put it alongside every other promise I've ever made to you. YOU WILL GET BETTER.

I love you,

Patrick

The girls and I have also learned a lot about how Patrick spent his days at work. He was very well-loved by patients and coworkers. I was amazed at how many people "got" his crazy sense of humor. He did drive some of them crazy, and I've enjoyed hearing those stories too! I could commiserate with his office manager, Jennifer, who tried to keep him in line during the day, since I wasn't around to do it. We knew he was good at his job, and I am so happy that my girls now have so much evidence of that.

ENTRY 20

GRIEF JOURNALS – MAY AND JUNE 2016

My friend, Sonia, went through a similarly awful experience when her husband, Kevin, died over a decade ago. Sonia brought journals for the girls and me after Patrick died, and I decided to start journaling.

5/7/16 — It's been 2 ½ weeks, and I still have a gaping hole in my heart. I can't believe you are gone. Sometimes, it just hits me like I was punched in the stomach. This wasn't supposed to happen. This doesn't happen to people we know. You were so alive and beautiful. How can you be gone? I don't remember the last time we made love.

I can't stop thinking about the actual impact. What part of you was hurt first? Did you feel it? What broke? Was there time for you to feel pain or worry? I hope with all my heart that it was quick. I wish I had spent more time saying goodbye to you. I just want to touch you again. I would love nothing more than to snuggle with you in bed. Oh my God, Patrick, you can't be gone! I can't do this!

We can get through anything because we are together. This was a mantra that we repeated throughout our marriage. Words that were once comforting to me now seemed hopeless. How would I get through this without him?

I have no clue how I will live without you! How should I feel about the accident? Should I sue the guy? Sometimes I don't think about him, and then I hate him. I'm not sure I can take care of myself and the girls.

Everything we do is going to make me so sad because you are not here. I loved you so much, but I feel like it wasn't enough. There are lots of what-ifs. What if we made love the night before? Would you have blown off your workout and slept in? What if you had gone for a run instead?

What do you want us to do now? What would make you happy and proud? Should I stay here? Move? Should I keep working? Too many decisions! I just want you back!

5/9/16 — It doesn't get any easier. I'm trying to distract myself, and I think I need to face the fact that you are gone. I have no clue how to do this. I think I'm doing it wrong. Why did this happen to us? Couldn't it happen to people who weren't happy? I loved you so much, baby, and I never expected to say goodbye this soon! The girls are having a hard time too. Camille got accepted to Camp Royal and doesn't want to go. I am really sad because it's a great opportunity, but I don't want to force her to go. And Sierra is registered for the LSAT. I'm not sure if she should take it as practice or not.

This next part is complicated and personal. I'm using a pseudonym for the former boyfriend who contacted me and provided emotional support. I dated him before Patrick, and it didn't end on the best terms, but I always thought of him affectionately. I'm including this because it was a huge part of my recovery. He lives far away, and our communication was mainly through messaging. My counselor told me that sometimes people show up at the right time for the right reason. He was there for me for a season, and we moved forward with our separate lives. I will say that, in hindsight, I was very vulnerable; like a drowning person, I was looking for someone to pull me up. He did that, but he was always a gentleman.

And I've been talking to Ted. It's very comforting, but I'm also feeling guilty about it. I just want to wake up and have this be a bad dream. And I also want some assurance that I will see you again. I believe in heaven, but things like this cause so much doubt. I have to go back to thinking that God was watching over me, and maybe that will help.

I know Patrick and God were watching over me the day Patrick died. I was looking for him, and I made it to the roadblock. As I tried to decide if I should get closer, I had an overwhelming feeling that I needed to go home. Nothing good would come out of me getting closer. God and Patrick guided me home to our daughter.

5/13/16 — I still can't believe you are gone. I want to know what happened to that guy who couldn't stand to be away from me? Did you really love me that much? Are you really gone? I'm having a hard time allowing myself to mourn. It seems like I feel little pricks. My breath catches, and it suddenly hits me that you are gone. I still think I will wake up and it will all be a bad dream. I am so worried about the girls. Sierra doesn't want to leave my room, and Camille just doesn't show a lot of emotion. I wish I were home alone because I feel like screaming hysterically.

I did find a way to scream hysterically without freaking anyone out. I had a grief playlist that was guaranteed to make me cry. I would get in the car, hit play, and drive to the crash site (I no longer call a preventable collision an accident). As I got closer, I would let out a guttural scream as loud as possible. I highly recommend this! I always felt better!

It's so unfair that you worked so hard and never got to enjoy retirement, and now I will probably be able to do more. Everyone wants to help, and there's NOTHING anyone can do. I don't understand at all. WHY DID THIS HAPPEN??!! You were so alive and so awesome, and you drove me crazy at times, but I loved you so much! I have so many regrets. I wish we had made love recently. I don't remember the last time, and I'm so sorry it wasn't more! I really want there to be a heaven because I can't stand the thought of never being with you again. I want Whoopi Goldberg to come speak for you!

5/20/16 — It's been an entire month, and I guess this is real. This is so fucking unfair!! I'm not sure I can survive this. I am really trying to feel you, and I can't. The accident was such a random combination of bad choices, none of which should have caused the accident, and the kid has probably had a bad life. What would you want to happen? Our life was just too perfect to end like this. And I don't know what the hell to do now. I can't even do basic activities. I guess I need to move forward, but I don't know how to do that. (At this point in the journal, the writing is smeared; I was clearly crying.) *The only way I am surviving is by living in this fantasy world with Ted. I know Ted has always loved me, and I feel like that's what I need. The circumstances suck, but I don't know. I wish that I could feel your arms around me. I wish I could tell you I loved you. I wish I would have kept myself in better shape. Thank you for always loving me anyway. And thank you for providing for the girls and me. I think we really will be okay.*

5/25/16 — It's a bad night. I still can't believe you are gone. I miss you so much! I wish I could just go back 30 years and live life with you one more time! It was a great life, and I just wish I had realized how precious it was. I know this Ted thing is a distraction, and I'm not sure I can keep doing it because I feel like I will get hurt. And why did I not save cards from you in recent years?! All of the cards from long ago mean so much to me. I really wish we had read the cards and letters together, maybe for an anniversary. I just would have enjoyed doing that with you. And damn it! I want a sign!! I want to know you are okay and that you still love me. I keep looking for something. It hurts so much, and it's just so unfair that you are gone! I love you so much! Random people reach out to me, and it's sweet, but none of them have any idea.

6/4/16 — I can't believe how long you've been gone! I am worried that I will start forgetting things about you. I am always trying to picture you and imagine your touch. We were so happy, and this is so unfair! There are so many unhappy couples. Why did God need you?? I just don't understand! Every day seems to get harder, and I miss you more. I still don't know how I am going to go on. How did this happen? Can you please show me a sign that you are okay, you love me, and I'm going to be okay? Can God let you do that? I am so sad.

6/6/16 — I miss you so much. I'm so sad, baby, and I just can't believe I didn't get to say goodbye. And I want to talk to you so badly. I just can't believe this happened. I'm not ready for our love story to be over. I don't want to be a widow. I don't want to move forward. I want to wake up from this horrible nightmare. I'm glad you didn't suffer, but I wish I could have said goodbye. Thank you so much for loving me and taking care of me for so long. I expected to grow old with you. I just don't even know how you are gone. You should be right here! Camille got her championship ring today, and she's very excited! Can't I just have one more day with you?

One more anniversary, or 25 more? (My writing appears less steady at this point, and I can tell there were more tears.) *Why? Why? Why? It's not fair! It's not fair! It's not fair!*

6/12/16 — It seems to get harder every day. I miss you so, so MUCH!! I wish I could feel your presence and dream about you. Maybe I am trying too hard? Grief is just consuming me. I wish I could just be in shock for the rest of my life. Shock was so much nicer. I don't like feeling the grief. I know you would not want to cause me pain. Damn it!! We were supposed to grow old together! I just can't find any peace. And I'm kind of mad at God right now.

My next entry is a poem I wrote.

I close my eyes, and I see
Your smile
A sweet smile at a glance
For me, it means so much more
The smile I get when I surprise you!
A smile for ME
A look of love
Our shared secret
I remember
I remember what it means
Your smile fills my heart
With love
I don't see it in the pictures
I can't find it
I feel it was a special smile
For me only
I want to burn it into my memory
To never forget
I will close my eyes again

Why did this have to happen? I hate this! This is not what we planned. We should have been getting ready for a party right now. Or probably we would be in Pismo with Matt and Tina. It's so hard to let myself FEEL this! I don't know how people survive this. I really don't. You were my whole world. It's so unfair!! I'm just going to stay right here. I want to hibernate and wake up healed.

The last entry has no date.

I miss you so much right now. My heart just doesn't want to believe you're gone. I can't believe this happened to me. To us! I try really hard just to remember the good times, but there are SO MANY that it hurts.

ENTRY 21

ONE NEEDS TO BE THE CLOWN – AUGUST 6, 2016

Patrick was always good with kids. I noticed this when we were dating, and I always knew he would be a great father. He wasn't as comfortable around babies and always said he wouldn't hold them until they could pass the "three-foot drop test!" Of course, I always wanted to be a mom, and I knew it would be part of the "Happily Ever After" I envisioned with Patrick.

Patrick and I dated for six years, so I didn't expect surprises when we attended the Engaged Encounter weekend our church required. As part of the weekend, we each had a notebook. We had sets of questions we would answer individually, and then we would meet and exchange notebooks. One of the questions was, "How many kids do you want and when?" I put "two to three in four to five years." Patrick put "NONE EVER." I pulled the priest over to discuss this because it was a deal breaker for me, and how did I date him for six years and miss this?!

Patrick admitted he feared he wouldn't be a good parent. I imagine he probably thought there was no way he could ever measure up to his parents because they are pretty awesome. I don't know why he didn't realize they had already taught him everything he needed to know!

We talked with the priest and agreed Patrick would eventually be okay with having kids.

I must clarify that the eulogy (see Appendix) made it sound like I tricked him into fatherhood. That was not the case. Although it took a while to bring him around, we had Sierra in four years as part of my master plan.

As he warmed up to the prospect of being a father, I remember him earnestly discussing the type of parents we would be. He said, "I think that in every family, one parent needs to be the disciplinarian, and one needs to be the clown." I didn't have to ask which one he planned to be!

By the time we decided to start a family, he was 100 percent on board and never looked back. He still worried about the three-foot drop test, but when a nurse handed Sierra to him in the delivery room, he held her as if she was the most precious thing he had ever held, and she was. When we brought her home, he got up with her during the night, changed her diaper, swaddled her like a pro, and then brought her to me to nurse.

Many women told me this was not normal behavior, but this was just the kind of husband and father he was. He also bought a cookbook and made all the baby food from scratch!

When I was pregnant with Camille, he wanted another daughter to dote on, and his wish came true. I had to go on a business trip for three days when Camille was two months old. Many people asked if I was worried about him being alone with the kids, which always made me laugh. He joked that it was easy because he had one less person to care for, which was probably true. He had the parent thing down, and I never worried.

Throughout their childhood, I must say the most important thing to us was to love and enjoy time with our girls. Our house was never spotless. Neither of us was much of a disciplinarian, and we were always surprised they turned out okay despite this.

As they got older, we had a lot of conversations where we talked about how amazing they were and how proud we were of them.

Patrick liked to say he had no idea why they turned out so well because we were crappy parents. I agreed that we couldn't take a lot of credit.

He fulfilled his promise to be the clown, and thank God the girls and I have many memories of that. I'm very grateful he was around for most of their childhood. A few weeks ago, I cried when I heard how well Camille had done on a test. I told my mother-in-law, Barbara, "Patrick would be so proud."

She reminded me, "He knows."

I will keep that in mind as I continue to move forward. I am 100 percent confident that Patrick wants us to be happy and have a good life. I'm trying hard to keep the humor alive, and luckily the "clown" taught his daughters all his tricks, so there are a lot of smiles and laughter around here.

Our family through the years, from 1999 to 2010

ENTRY 22

The girls left today for a beach vacation with Denny and his kids. I could have joined them tomorrow, but I thought having a short trial of being alone would be good. I can't remember the last time I was alone for this long. I have another year with Camille, but eventually I will push her out of the nest and watch her soar, so I need to start preparing myself.

I am very sad to say I had once been nervous about the thought of Patrick and I being empty nesters. The girls had been the center of our lives for 21 years. Would we drive each other crazy? Would it be hard just to be the two of us again?

Seriously? I really thought that? I would give anything for that to be my future right now.

Over the years, we tried to take time away from the girls, but we loved being a family so much that we rarely went away alone. We had several great anniversary trips: Madonna Inn, the Inn at Avila Beach, Kon Tiki Inn, and Tenaya Lodge. We did try to make time alone, and we definitely had good times.

Right now, I can't even fathom living alone after Camille graduates. Being alone was so *not* the plan. To say this is not how I expected things to turn out is such an understatement.

When I lost Patrick, I also lost other unexpected things. I've heard these are called "secondary losses." The biggest one is just being a part of a couple. I mean, everywhere you look, there are couples! And they usually do annoying things like hold hands, smile at each other, etc. I never realized that being part of a couple was such a big part of my identity, but I feel the loss acutely.

I lost my companion, my occasional dinner date. I lost the person I discussed *everything* with, the first person I would go to if I had a problem. I lost the father of my children, my co-parent. The kids are mostly grown, but any decisions left to be made are squarely on my shoulders.

I lost the guy who knew everything about the yard, the pool, and other household things. I lost my physical therapist and masseuse. I'm sure he would laugh because it was *not* his favorite job! I know I drove him crazy, but he took good care of me.

I also lost a walking encyclopedia of knowledge and memories. I don't know how he remembered so many things, but it was nice because I didn't have to. I can't tell you how often I have needed information that only he has. We still don't know where the pipes are and Matt had to guess how to finish Patrick's last batch of beer because we couldn't find the beer journal. And, yeah, we all lost the clown, the source of so many smiles and laughter.

So now I am learning to be alone. I have a whole army of friends and family who want to protect me from being alone, but I must be able to do this at the end of the day. That's the irony of this situation. Everyone wants to fix this, and no one can. Only time will ease the pain. I know I can do it, and I promise I will survive, but right now, I still can't wrap my mind around the fact that he is gone.

ENTRY 23

THE BEST-KEPT SECRET – AUGUST 13, 2016

Guess what I have learned? You can't wrap grief up in a nice little package and make it disappear. This surprised me because no one wants to talk about it. Death is an uncomfortable subject, so it is easier to pretend it is unpleasant, but then you move on. I don't see people walking around teary-eyed months or years after losing someone, so it must be okay after a while.

The traditional mourning period used to last for an entire year, which is depressing. So somewhere along the way, society decided it was better just to move on as quickly as possible. The reality is that it's just not that simple.

Grief is really, really hard. This is the secret no one tells you. I always thought it would be difficult at first, but that I would recover quickly and move forward because that's how it works, right? I've watched more than one movie where someone has lost a spouse. There is a common scene where they sit watching a wedding video or a movie about happier times. And they are inconsolable. Sometimes, this scene repeats a few times, but eventually, they recover and move on to whatever the movie's point is. It's all nice and neat.

I have tried watching my wedding video. I really want to watch the whole long thing because we have lost a lot of people in the last year, and I am pretty sure most of them are in the video. I can make it through the first part, which is kind of like a music video (the soundtrack is "Just Like Heaven" by The Cure), and I was able to watch it up to the first reading, but I haven't gotten past that. Watching it night after night? No, thank you.

I still cannot wrap my mind around the fact that Patrick is gone. What has surprised me is that, after almost four months, my mind still plays games with me. I continue to have daily conversations with myself like this:

"He's not gone!"

"Yes, he is, remember [INSERT ANY AWFUL MEMORY]?"

"Oh yeah, that *did* happen."

I don't know why, but I had no idea it would be like this.

Most days, I feel like I am making progress; I can pull myself up, start a project, go on a fun trip, etc. Then I do something simple like checking my email and seeing an email from the US Mint advertising their latest commemorative coins. No big deal, right? *Wrong*! Patrick collected these coins. They were one of the few things on his Christmas list every year. The man wanted *nothing* and would get mad if I bought him too many presents. So I loved buying the latest coins for him.

I also have trouble walking down the beer aisle in stores. I don't like beer, but Patrick *loved* beer. And I knew just what he liked. There are always a lot of microbrewery IPAs in large bottles with really cool pictures and names. My favorite was Arrogant Bastard Pale Ale. I would tell him I found the perfect beer for him! I always knew I would get a great smile if I came home with beer.

I will never forget Patrick. There is no way to really "get over" this. I do think as time goes on, there will be more smiles and fewer tears. Grieving will be a lifelong process, and that's okay. As I've said before, I choose to celebrate Patrick and the life he lived. I hope people are never afraid to bring up Patrick around me.

They can tell me they care. They can tell me funny stories. And if they're grieving too, I hope they share that with me; it's good for both of us!

ENTRY 24

I would like to make a public service announcement for all married couples who know they need a will, but they're not planning on dying, so there is no rush, right? They'll do it someday. Who wants to talk about death? That's no fun! Guess when it's *really* not fun to talk about it? When you no longer have the chance to discuss it with your spouse!

The first conversation can be about wills. Patrick and I did not have wills. In my situation, it hasn't presented any problems. We were each other's beneficiaries, so it wasn't that complicated. However, if something had happened to both of us, it would have been more difficult for the girls. I was actually surprised by the number of policies and insurance plans we had in his name. His former coworkers told me about a VA pension, and I discovered that I was paying for an accidental death and dismemberment policy in addition to the one he had. By the way, you should always enroll in any free life insurance or accidental death policies that are frequently included on credit cards or bank accounts. I thought I had a small policy through my credit union, but I had never enrolled.

I am now going through the process of finalizing my will. It will say what I want to do with everything, and also record all the essential information. I am paying to have it done because my brain is scrambled, but there are a lot of websites where anyone can do it themselves and just get it notarized.

Getting a will done isn't something to procrastinate about, especially when children are involved.

Next, final wishes and funeral plans. Again, not a fun conversation. I'm actually kind of glad Patrick and I didn't have our last wishes in writing. Patrick hated funerals. He didn't want any money spent on him. Put him in a cardboard box, etc. To be clear, when we discussed dying, I told him that if he died first, I would do whatever I wanted. I said to him that funerals were for the living. If we had a long life together, I probably would have been okay with doing it differently, but in an unexpected and tragic situation, you are looking for what seems best for those left behind. So have conversations about death. Try to honor each other's wishes, but maybe give your spouse your blessing to do what comforts them the most.

I also suggest you look at what each of you handles in the household. For example, I paid all the bills, and almost everything was electronic. Patrick would have had no clue what to do if I had died first. I had an agreement with my friend Lisa that we would help each other's spouses if one of us were to die, but I never gave her essential info, such as passwords, so it still would have been nearly impossible! In my case, if I hadn't been the one handling the bills, I would not have had passwords to the accounts, which would have made the tasks more difficult.

So please, have the uncomfortable conversations! And do it sooner rather than later. Patrick knew many things that would have made things easier for me. I am slowly figuring it out, but just handle it now if you can!

ENTRY 25

Yesterday, I noticed the calendar on the side of my fridge out of the corner of my eye. Patrick liked to have it there to record important dates. I record everything on my phone and never use the calendar, so I suspected it was probably still on April, and I was right. I thought that made perfect sense. Time stopped in April in many ways, and moving past what happened is complicated.

On the other hand, I have realized I have much to be thankful for. I never want to say anything good happened "because Patrick died." There is nothing positive about the fact that he is gone. I guess a better way to put it is, in addition to all the sadness, I've experienced a lot of good since he died.

I am incredibly grateful for my family—the whole huge extended Boyles, Hatch, teNyenhuis, and Prandini clan! I have three siblings and over 20 cousins. Patrick had four siblings and over 30 cousins! And they are all very close families. As we get older, keeping track of everyone's growing families is more challenging, and we just don't spend as much time together. Now my immediate families have almost merged. Sierra and Camille used to have trouble keeping track of everyone. In the days immediately following Patrick's death, as we spent time with extended family, they regularly quizzed me about how everyone fit in. They have a good handle on it now and have told me they enjoy seeing everyone more often. We have been having extended family get-togethers on the first Friday of each month.

Family was very important to Patrick, and we all agree he would be thrilled that we are spending more time together.

Sierra, Camille, and I have discovered inner strength we didn't know we had. Camille was a rock and went back to school the week after the service. She finished her school year by excelling at her AP tests and doing exceptionally well on the SAT. She did exactly what her dad would have done. Sierra became my protector and sounding board. She had planned to move to a new apartment over the summer, so we had rented a storage unit. We returned to Long Beach to move her belongings the week after the service. While there, she interviewed for a spot on the moot court team and was selected. The California State University Long Beach team is very successful, and she will get to travel with them to tournaments, including one here in Fresno. Being on the team will help her as she prepares to apply to law school.

I have found an increased sense of confidence. For years, I have felt that I failed at teaching, which is what I went to college for, and didn't always feel I had purpose at my current insurance job. I would not have thought I could get through this sudden loss. I have discovered that staying calm in a traumatic situation is a strength I possess. I am currently researching how I might use that in my future career. I am beginning to make plans to return to school, probably in psychology or counseling. This vision was not in my dreams before, and is a little exciting!

I also continue to appreciate my almost 30 years with this wonderful man! Many people don't ever get to experience the kind of relationship we had. When I start getting sad, I try to pull up one of my many happy memories, which usually gets me through.

Every day is still challenging, but I am grateful for occasional bright spots!

ENTRY 26

I've been trying to do some organizing and decluttering. I feel that less clutter will help me feel better. Patrick and I were both kind of pack rats. I think that comes from growing up without a lot of excess belongings.

Neither of us wanted to get rid of something we might need at some point. Patrick pretended not to be a pack rat, but I found 10 to 15 pairs of used insoles in his shoe bin, so the proof is there! Now I'm trying to eliminate some of the nonessential stuff.

Sometimes, it just seems like there is not a place for everything that I want to keep, and this is the reason we had clutter to begin with. Ironically, I now have some extra space for things if I want to use them: a dresser, a nightstand, and half of a closet.

Seriously though, I have not thrown out his toothbrush. It's funny how some things are easy to let go of. I had no problem bidding farewell to the insoles. I cleaned the bathroom cabinets this weekend and removed most of his shaving creams, lotions, etc. His deodorant is in a sealed bag with a few T-shirts I pulled out of the laundry. I figured it would help preserve the familiar scent. But I can't seem to let go of the toothbrush. There's just something comforting about it being there.

His wallet still has $10 in it. I know he won't have an opportunity
to spend it, but I didn't want to take it. In typical Patrick style, he
didn't carry a lot of money. He probably wanted to be able to say
he didn't have the cash to get me a Diet Pepsi! So I always made
sure he had some in there.

And the clothes. I can't imagine walking into my closet and not
having them in there. I let several cousins and nephews pick out
shirts to wear to the service and keep. Giving his belongings to
someone else makes it easier to let go. We are planning to make
quilts out of his T-shirts and flannels. I know why I am attached to
those. He never willingly got rid of any T-shirt!

You could find him in the yard on any weekend in a stained
T-shirt with holes. He didn't want to ruin any of his "good" shirts.
The shirt he wore in the "Blackbird" video was a gift from my
mom, and is at least 25 years old! It was also in the laundry basket,
so it's now in the sealed bag. I'm sure any of his friends or family
could describe at least one of his shirts because he wore them
repeatedly.

I am finding other things to clear out for now. Eventually, it will be
easier to let go of more, but I know there is no timetable for this,
and even if there were, I don't care. I'll do it at my own pace—a
little at a time. Grief is just not very good company. I let it visit
occasionally, since it's the right thing to do. Then I think of something crazy Patrick did or said, and grief vanishes for a while.

ENTRY 27

The stages of grief have been on my mind. I have experienced most of them, but not in a neat, orderly fashion. And I am beginning to suspect that you never really get through any of them.

Although I didn't realize it then, I now believe I was, initially, in shock for a *long* time. Reflecting on the initial days and weeks, I almost feel like I am watching a scene from someone else's life. I functioned at minimum capacity. I let others help me with the things I could not do. I was in pain, but had not even begun to *feel* the loss. They say denial is one of the first stages. At the time, I thought I was doing pretty well. I knew he was gone.

The funny thing is, my mind is no longer in denial, but my heart is. I seem to have these inner arguments, with the mind stating the facts and the heart saying, "It is JUST. NOT. POSSIBLE." At some point, they will come to some sort of agreement, but right now, my heart is winning. So denial is an ongoing stage.

That day seems to run on an endless loop in my head. I study it and try to comprehend how I got through. If I start to feel happy, my mind says, "Wait, maybe you haven't seen this movie?" And then the facts are laid out before me, and I know he's really gone. I'm not looking for sympathy or pity. I assume that most people going through grief are hurting too. I just never imagined grief was like this.

I have experienced some anger. A little at the person who caused this. I'm mainly indifferent to him because I just can't waste any emotions on him right now. I have also been irrationally angry at Patrick. Why did he have to be so devoted to working out? How could he leave me? I do realize that this was not a choice he made. Mainly, I am just mad at the universe. He was too young to die.

The depression stage comes and goes.

This last week, I've been very emotional. I have good days and bad days, but I missed Patrick this week. It's still hard to comprehend going through life without him. I had a hectic weekend and saw a lot of friends and family, which helped pull me back up. And while I was sad, I let myself cry often. I think it's good, and I always feel a little better.

I think acceptance is kind of elusive. And really, why would you ever want to accept losing someone you love? Maybe it should be called resignation instead? I guess it is just going to take time to deal with all of the different emotions. I wish there were a short-cut through grief. Unfortunately, we must go through all of it to move forward—one step at a time.

ENTRY 28

Recently I reviewed my social profile descriptions. They all say the same thing: "I am a happily married mother of two." I just can't bring myself to change them. Who would I be, then?

One of the hardest parts of losing your spouse is losing part of your identity. I'm not ready to embrace the term "widow," but I get annoyed when it is not an option on paperwork, because I'm definitely not single. And I may never change my relationship status on Facebook. Widow is such a sad term, and I don't like doing the sad thing!

I've been shredding old paperwork, and I got rid of all of "our" address labels. Today, I wondered if I should save some of the paperwork from our early life together, such as canceled checks, bank statements, and doctors' bills. I do not need any of these things, but shredding them was a really odd feeling. I saved a few checks to have a copy of his signature.

There are still a lot of things in both of our names. I've only changed what I had to. I'm in no rush to change them all. I feel like it's a step forward each time I do something like that, but there is no timeline for getting it all done. I realize I'm still the same person I was on April 19. I will always be Patrick's wife. And I'm still a mother of two.

Unhappily widowed? Tragically widowed? I'll just leave the happily married part for now.

ENTRY 29

Today, I was looking up something on Google Maps and decided to look at Google Street View. I pulled up my house, and it seemed to be a recent picture. I know Patrick was alive when it was taken because the lawn was freshly mown in his signature diagonal style. I found a sort of date stamp, and it said April 2016. I became obsessed with trying to find out exactly when it was taken! I could tell it was morning, but I was puzzled that my car was not in front. I knew it wasn't taken after he died, because no vehicles were in front of my house.

From April 20 until at least the end of the month, my street had always looked like a party was going on. When I talked to a neighbor across the street, she said she thought we were having a graduation party. In April? For a week and a half? 24/7? If only that were the case.

I am constantly looking for remnants of Patrick's life. I always hope that I will find some small part of him. Today, I discovered his juggling set, including some sort of knives! I'm glad he never tried to teach the girls. I also found a box containing the contents of his desk at the VA. There was a Rolodex, a new pair of insoles, a yellow rain poncho, a custom-made mouse pad of the "teNyenhuis girls" I had forgotten about, and a photo album of baby pictures. I was happy he had a whole photo album and remembered how proud he always was of his girls.

As usual, I felt incomplete when I finished looking through the box. I am never going to find something that replaces Patrick. I'm also not going to stop wishing I could step into one of those pictures and go back and enjoy my life even more than I did the first time. I try not to have regrets, but I also think I did not fully appreciate our love and marriage as a beautiful gift. At the same time, my heart warms every time I find a new artifact from our relationship. We *did* have a great life together. That life is over, but my life continues. I just need to keep heading toward my new normal.

ENTRY 30

I found something else when I was searching in the garage. I found a box of things from high school and college. I am sentimental, so I save a lot of stuff like that. The box mostly had certificates and sports award programs. Many items were from my cross-country and track years at Clovis High. There were also writing assignments from high school and college, poems I had written, and some free-form journaling. I've been writing a lot since Patrick died, but I am still surprised that I had forgotten how much I used to write when I was younger!

In high school, I spent a lot of time journaling or writing poems if something bothered me. I continued writing at the beginning of college. I met Patrick in the summer of 1986. He was home from University of the Pacific for the summer, and I was on summer break from Fresno State. We began what would be a six-year, long-distance relationship. Back then, we did not have cell phones or email. Long-distance calls could be costly, and we were broke college students. So we sent each other a *lot* of cards and letters!

I am eternally grateful to have a written history of our early relationship. Right after Patrick died, when I was still in a semi-state of shock, I began reading through these letters. I would read a few at a time, sorting them into two Ziplock bags in case the girls ever choose to read them. One bag is labeled "PG," and the other has a warning, as they might not like the content. I had to put them away as the shock began to wear off. I will read the rest someday, but it's just too hard right now.

As I read through them, it occurred to me that I would have enjoyed reading through them with Patrick. I think it would have been a great way to reconnect and reminisce. Relationships fail because the early days are exhilarating, but it is not like that forever. Your love matures, and you become more comfortable with each other. When the "honeymoon" period is over, a relationship becomes something that you have to nurture. You can't take it for granted. There will be give and take; it won't be as picture-perfect as your courtship and honeymoon. Patrick and I always seemed to find ways to rekindle that love, but I wish I had thought of the letters.

And the letters were not all hearts and roses either. One letter from Patrick was a heartbreaker! He had been dating another girl at University of the Pacific, and when he initially returned to school after the summer we met, he was torn between the two of us. In the letter, Patrick told me that he loved both of us, but was choosing her over me because he didn't think he could have a long-distance relationship. I, of course, knew better, and we all know how that ended! I had forgotten about this particular letter, but I wasn't upset reading it. That was part of our story; after that, I was always confident in our relationship.

People have said this for decades, but writing is a lost art. We are all bombarded with constant communication. My children interact with their friends way more than I did, but much of it consists of short text conversations, Snapchat stories, and other social media posts. That doesn't mean they are not close, but when they eventually start having serious relationships, I hope they also record their thoughts and feelings in something more permanent than a text.

I challenge you to take the time to send a card or letter to someone you care about. It doesn't need to be long. Just let your loved one know how much they mean to you. As I thought of this last night, I wrote each of the girls a letter. And by writing, I mean I typed it in a document on my phone and emailed it to them. I'm a modern mom, right?

My favorite find was a card Patrick sent me when I moved into our first apartment, shortly before we were married. The card said, "I Miss You." Inside, Patrick wrote: "Danell, I'm so happy that I will never have to send you another card like this. I love you! Pat." The card pretty much sums up how excited we were for the long-distance part of the relationship to end. I have so many good memories, and I am thankful I was blessed to be his wife!

ENTRY 31

As my kids were growing up, I loved to share funny stories with my mom. She always laughed and told me I needed to write them down. I didn't have a blog back then. I'm sure that I intended to write them down, but why would I need to? I was married to a man who could remember everything!

I didn't realize at first how many memories we lost. I'm unsure why, but my brain doesn't always store details. I remember a lot, but Patrick could remember obscure things, such as lines from movies I had never heard of.

Like everything else, I think he trained his brain to do this. After college, he never truly learned to read for pleasure. I know he enjoyed reading, but it had to be something of value. He read the entire Bible, and when he finished, he chose to read the biographies of each of the presidents. I think he made it to Reagan and then stopped. He decided the biographies were more accurate after time had passed. The more recent ones were usually written by supporters and tended to be sugar-coated. Of course, I can't think of any cool facts, but he loved to share odd things he had learned, such as the president who took calls while on the toilet!

He was also great at telling jokes. I would try to repeat them, and they were never quite as funny. A highlight of Steam Donkeys shows was the jokes and banter between songs, much of it groan-worthy! I am so grateful that I have videos of that. Usually, I can get through them with a smile.

He had favorite sayings too; we have forgotten some of them. He used to tell us that our house had only two rules. Rule 1 is: Never Throw Things from the Second Floor, but we are unsure of Rule 2. Rule 2 could be that Dad is Awesome (which he frequently said) or that Dad Is Always Right. Maybe it was Dad Needs a Beer.

Of course, like anyone, he didn't remember everything, especially if it was a message his wife was supposed to give him! He would be talking to his mom, and she would say, "I'm sure Danell told you . . . " and he would tell her, "You know we never talk." In fairness, I would say the same thing.

He had another saying related to irony—I think it was poetic irony—but it seems like it was a more obscure term. When he found an example of this type of irony, he loved to tell us. Recently, I experienced this type of irony, and although it was a little sad, I could just imagine him laughing at the irony of the situation.

A month or two after Patrick died, I charged my old iPhone to see if I had any voice messages from him. There had been none on my current phone. I found one message from 2013. He had been on some sort of weekend adventure, and I was gone when he got home. He left me a message to say he was home, exhausted, and going to sleep. He ended it with "I love you." I tried to save the message, but the older phone did not have the option to do that. So, rather than playing the message on the old phone and recording it with the new one, I had the brilliant idea of updating it. Of course, when the update was complete, my messages were gone. I took it to the phone store, and they confirmed there was no way to retrieve it. I was sad, but I wasn't going to let myself be devastated about it. At the same time, I was still searching to ensure I didn't miss any audio or video recordings. Eventually, I found the voice memos on my phone.

Wouldn't it be sweet if he had recorded me a message? I found an 18-second message, which was very staticky at first. After a minute, I realized I had made the recording myself. In the middle of the night. When his snoring woke me up! I'm unsure what I planned to do with it, but I never shared it with him. He was sensitive about snoring, and his feelings would have been hurt. I burst into laughter! How ironic! I'm looking for a sweet message, and instead I find the snoring I had recorded in anger. Now that's (insert term) irony!

By the way, I was persistent and eventually found a way to retrieve that voicemail from my computer!

ENTRY 32

I drove a 26-foot U-Haul truck today. While driving, it occurred to me that I would never have done this when Patrick was alive. To be fair, I didn't have to drive it today. The plan was for Denny to drive the U-Haul, but it made more sense for me to, since it needed to be parked at my house tonight. Denny was hosting our monthly "First Friday" get-together, so it made more sense for him to get home. He will drive it up the curving foothill roads to Burrough Valley tomorrow so we can move my mom and stepdad, Ernie, into town. He doesn't want to do it either, but that's what brothers are for!

I have learned to do a lot of things that I never had to do before. I have cleaned the pool filter at least 10 times and spent many hours brushing the sides and skimming leaves off the top. I changed the handle on the toilet. I cleaned the dog's ears. I drove Patrick's VW bus. Okay, I didn't drive it, but I pulled it out of the garage and back in.

I have also done things I knew how to do but never had to do before. I am now the scooper of dog poop—a job Patrick hated and complained about regularly. And yeah, I probably should have done it sooner, but I never had to. I do the grocery shopping occasionally, LOL. I still don't cook much, but I'm trying to cook more. There are countless other things that I just never had to do, but there is no reason why I can't do them now.

I put registration tags on my car and his bus. I've done this before, but usually I just had him do it. He really could do just about anything. I'm amazed I can even function without him, but I know he is my guardian angel! That is why I feel I can do just about anything now. That doesn't mean I don't occasionally dissolve into tears if I can't immediately figure something out. The pool has made me cry several times, and I felt pretty helpless when the smoke alarm in the attic needed a new battery (thank you, Denny, for climbing up there to replace it). At the same time, I like it when I can figure things out for myself. I think it makes me feel like I am going to be okay.

We will really miss him tomorrow. He was very strong and would have been an enormous help. Plus, he would have spent the day joking around with Denny and Tom, making the move more entertaining. And I know he would have driven the U-Haul for us!

ENTRY 33

WHAT IF WE NEVER MET? - OCTOBER 9, 2016

Last night, I was utterly exhausted from a day of moving my mom and Ernie. I hadn't slept well the night before, so I should have slept like a log. Of course, as usual, I woke several times during the night, which is kind of my new normal. Just to clarify, this doesn't mean I wake up crying and in emotional pain. Patrick is always in the back of my mind, but the pain seems to be a little better most days. When I was awake last night, I started thinking about something that I thought about a *lot* at first.

When the pain was the most intense, there were times that I prayed for amnesia. I just wanted not to remember. And I considered if it would be better to go through life kind of happy rather than experiencing the extreme pain of losing Patrick. I've been told that "most people" don't experience the type of love and happiness I had. What if I didn't have that? Of course, I always shut down this line of thinking because I would not have had our two precious daughters if I never met Patrick. And, of course, I wouldn't want to erase my time with him. My life was better because of it.

My life was incredibly enriched when I met Patrick. Mom and Pop—or Nona and Opa, as the kids call them—are the best in-laws anyone could ever have. They genuinely consider me their child, and I am so blessed to be a part of their family. Patrick's oldest brother, Dan, is like a big brother to me. He brought his wife, Amy, into my life, and even though they are far away, I cherish our relationship. His younger brother, Gabe, was always around during my college years when Patrick was away, and he looked out for me. I consider him Camille's surrogate father for education, and he's as proud of her as Patrick would be. Gabe's wife, Jen, is a kindred spirit, and I love having her in my life.

And Patrick gave me my own little sister, Dina. I love her so much, and I understand my sisters wanting to protect me from the pain I'm going through because I wish I could take away Dina's pain. She was extremely close to Patrick, and when she married Jeff, he found an outdoorsy buddy. Jeff and Dina were always ready to go fishing, hiking, or drinking beer with Patrick!

When I met Patrick's youngest sibling, Matt, he was 10 years old. So I've known him for much of his life, and Patrick was always proud of him. In many ways, he was truly Patrick's best friend. I've always been close to his wife, Tina, too. Like all of the siblings, Matt chose well!

Getting together with the whole family was always a special time. Holidays were always busy, but we always agreed on which family we would spend time with—*both*!

And that is just the tip of the iceberg, since the family doesn't end there. There are numerous nieces, nephews, cousins, etc., and my life is richer because of all of them. I still get extremely sad sometimes, and when that happens, if I start to wish that someone could just take away my memories, I think about all I would lose with them. I wouldn't give up the memories or my family!

ENTRY 34

LOOSE ENDS – OCTOBER 13, 2016

I've felt normal for a while. Not that I forgot what was going on, but I was feeling a little happy, not so sad. Last week, grief found me again, and I pushed it back, but I can only ignore it for so long. So I write.

Tonight, I am grateful for Cathy, who is always there when I need her. Earlier, I needed some company, and she knew without me even asking. Some days are just unexpectedly bad. And I know I have a long list of people who would be here if needed, but a best friend is nice. She knows she doesn't have to comfort me. She doesn't agonize over what to say because she knows all I need is her company.

I feel like there are so many loose ends in my life. I have no control over many of them, and I am just not ready to deal with some. I feel better when some are resolved, and others don't go as planned.

I finalized my will and trust a few weeks ago. Having a will may seem strange to be happy about, but it comforts me that everything is spelled out for the girls should anything happen to me. They also took care of the paperwork for the title on the house, which is good. The title now lists me as Danell teNyenhuis, an unmarried woman. That's so bizarre to me. I think I took 18 months to plan my wedding—a joyful, happy occasion. And then in an instant, almost 24 years later, I became unmarried. It is better than saying widowed, but it is just so odd. I still feel like I will wake up and realize it was all a dream.

Matt is now the official owner of Patrick's VW bus. It's still parked in my garage for now, but I am happy he is taking it. He has been introduced to Burnett's Auto Repair and they will continue taking care of the bus. Patrick loved that bus, and would be pleased that his little brother would use it and enjoy it. Matt has already taken the kids camping several times, so they are making lots of new memories.

I finally got the trees trimmed in the backyard, so I should be able to spend less time dealing with the pool. I am relieved to have three big things resolved and, hopefully, as I continue to check things off my list, my life will feel a little less chaotic.

ENTRY 35

OUR LAST WEEK TOGETHER – OCTOBER 17, 2016

When you lose someone you love, you spend much time replaying the last days you spent with them. I wish I had written things down sooner, since I'm sure I have forgotten some of them.

Patrick turned 49 one week before he died. A few months before that, I had heard that Paul McCartney would be in Fresno for the first time ever—and on Patrick's birthday. On March 16, the tickets went on sale, and I had the following text exchange with Patrick.

> Me: Happy Birthday! I love you!
>
> Patrick: Is it your boyfriends birthday or something?
>
> Me: Oops. Wrong lover.
>
> Me: No really, happy birthday to you! BEST WIFE EVER
>
> Me: Date night on your birthday.
>
> Patrick: I'm still getting these.
>
> Me: I know. Do you want to go out on April 13th?
>
> Patrick: On a Wednesday. Probably not.
>
> Me: We could go down a long and winding road.

Me: That leads to your door.

Patrick: You didn't!

Me: I DID

Patrick: I love you!

Initially, I bought two tickets. But later, I bought two more for the girls. Sierra would come home from Long Beach for Patrick's birthday and stay through the weekend.

On the big day, Patrick wanted to go to The Mad Duck for dinner since they had a great beer selection, but we called them on the way, and they were already super busy.

So we went to the Elephant Lounge, an Indian restaurant. We were relieved it was mostly empty as we drove into the parking lot. There was one small car in the front. Someone said it was good the restaurant wasn't crowded, and Camille (looking at the small car) said, "Oh, but there's a clown convention in town." Patrick beamed with pride. He was almost as proud of the girls' sense of humor as he was of their other accomplishments.

Dinner was great. We took pre-concert pictures, including my last picture ever with Patrick. While we were enjoying some naan bread, Sierra began singing "Naan, naan, naan, naan, naan, naan, hey, hey, hey. . . " We all laughed, and Patrick beamed with pride again.

Patrick and me, April 13, 2016

There were long lines when we got to the concert, so we waited quite a while, but Patrick kept us entertained. We took a picture of Patrick and the girls that I love and another of Patrick acting goofy, imitating the concert poster of Paul McCartney.

Sierra, Patrick, and Camille

Patrick mimicking Paul McCartney

When we finally got inside, the girls headed to their seats. Since I had purchased tickets at separate times, our seats weren't all together, but we texted each other pictures of the view. The girls were much closer to the stage!

Thirty minutes after the scheduled concert start time, Patrick began to say that it was very unprofessional that the concert was starting so late and that if the show didn't start in the next ten minutes, we were leaving. Being upset about the concert starting late was kind of a typical Patrick thing. I hoped he wouldn't go, but there was no way I was leaving. I knew the girls wouldn't leave either. Luckily, the concert started, and we had a great time!

I don't remember everything we did over the next few days, but Camille had a track meet on Saturday, so we watched that. We hated saying goodbye to Sierra on Sunday, but we knew the semester was almost over, and we would see her again soon.

On Monday, we had the Clovis East girls soccer awards dinner. The awards dinner was a little later than usual due to our postseason games and Valley Championship win. We had a lovely time, and the girls got a lot of recognition. Coach Jasara said some nice things about Camille, and she had special Valley Champion jackets made for the team (they would later wear them to the funeral).

That week, I had two online Jamberry nail sticker parties. I wasn't in the habit of painting my nails, but these were easy to use, so I had recently started selling them to get discounts on the ones I wanted to buy. One customer had questions, and I offered to take her a sample. When I learned she was leaving that Saturday for a cruise, I decided she needed a complete set of Jams! On Tuesday we had to pick up Patrick's VW bus from Burnett's Auto Repair. Patrick drove my car to work and then picked me up so I could take him to get the bus. On the ride there, I told him how much fun I was having with Jamberry. I had no expectations of getting rich, but it brought me much joy. He was happy that I was happy.

That night, after dinner, I went to the customer's house and had a pleasant visit with her while I showed her how to apply the nail wraps. As I drove home, I made plans with Cathy to meet at Mickey's Yogurt, since we knew they had our favorite flavor, Oatmeal Cookie Gelato. I took a picture of Cathy enjoying hers and sent it to Camille to tease her. Of course, she would know I would bring some home to her! I look at that picture occasionally, and it's surreal that I was having such a good evening, and the next day Patrick was gone!

When I got home, I remember Camille doing homework in the family room, and Patrick watching TV in the living room and enjoying a beer. Or two. I remember telling him what a great evening I had, but I don't think it was a particularly long conversation. I went into the family room with Camille and stayed up late, scheduling Facebook posts for my parties so they would post throughout the day while I was working. Patrick went to bed at some point and said good night on his way. He was asleep when I went to bed, and I didn't wake him. When I woke up Wednesday, he was already gone, not just from the house, but from my entire life.

I am so grateful we made so many memories that final week. I'm pleased Sierra was home for five days and we all had so much fun at the concert. And, of course, Patrick came home from the show and learned to play "Blackbird." At some point he recorded it, and I will cherish that video for the rest of my life!

ENTRY 36

I STILL CAN'T BELIEVE HE IS GONE - OCTOBER 20, 2016

I have had six months without Patrick, and I still can't believe he's gone. I say that to myself almost every day, and I don't want to dwell on that, but seriously, I am still trying to process his death.

I'm also moving forward. A few weeks ago, I received unexpected news. Aetna is offering early retirement packages if your age and years of service add up to 65, so I qualify! I am still off work and have been trying to decide when or if I could return, but I knew I would ultimately quit, so this is a huge blessing! I still need formal approval, but if everything goes according to plan, I could retire in early 2017 with an extended salary continuation! I have enrolled in an online master's in professional counseling program at Grand Canyon University.

Returning to school was the furthest thing from my mind six months ago. Retiring wouldn't have been an option. I am so blessed that Patrick's planning and Aetna's program allowed me to make this change. I consider it a gift from Patrick, and I hope that going into a helping profession will be an excellent way to honor him. He touched many lives, and I hope I can do the same.

ENTRY 37

A BREAK IN THE CLOUDS – OCTOBER 31, 2016

The cloud hanging over me has cleared for now. I have been waiting so long for the resolution of the case against the driver who hit Patrick, and the arraignment was today. The next court date is exactly one month away. I wasn't hoping for any particular thing to happen. I just wanted the waiting to be over.

I never know how I am going to react to updates. I don't remember when we got the first full update on the case, but it was sometime in May. I came home and locked myself in my room. I have only done that a few times. Sometimes, no amount of comfort helps. I only stayed there for 30 minutes to an hour, but felt like I would never calm down.

Over the summer, I had waited weeks between updates. The wheels of justice turn slowly, and you don't want them to take shortcuts anyway. I only shared earlier updates with family members because I was asked not to discuss the case publicly until the investigation was completed. Then, a few weeks ago, I met with the DA and received unexpected news on the case and went into a tailspin again. I was informed that the charge would likely be a misdemeanor (more on that later), not a felony like we expected. I couldn't even update anyone like I usually did. I only have to tell one person, and they can spread the word. But we have a lot of immediate family, so it's a lot of texting or calling.

I've been calmer since then. I was prepared to be a wreck the day I went to the DA's office. Ultimately, I felt they were just as diligent as the police, and I was okay after that meeting. I voted for the DA, Lisa Smittcamp, and am happy I made that choice. She is very dedicated and caring.

The arraignment was hard. I didn't know how to feel when I saw the defendant for the first time in person. The defendant pleaded not guilty. We did not expect the judge to increase the bail, so it was a small victory when he did. I had a lot of support in the courtroom with me, including our moms, Denise, Dawan, Denny, Connor, Cathy, Dina, Gabe, and Jen. I am never alone in this, and am very grateful for my family. And honestly, they wouldn't be anywhere else because they are all grieving too. As I have said from the beginning, I am surrounded by love.

ENTRY 38

Patrick used to go away once or twice a year for a weekend of camping, fishing, relaxing, and drinking beer. He often went with his "only friend," Joe, or his brother, Matt. I'm not going to lie; I think it was good to have a break. The girls and I would usually go and buy sugary cereal (he refused to buy that for them) and whatever other special treats they wanted. I would sleep well, since there was no snoring. After a day or two, I would start to miss him, and it was always nice when he got home. I saw his picture tonight and remembered how much I miss him. I don't need any more breaks; I just want him home.

At a wedding this weekend, I talked to relatives I hadn't seen since the funeral. My cousin, Steve, commented that he knew it hadn't hit me then, and he asked how long it was before it hit me. I told him it was probably a couple of months.

The initial shock is a blessing and a curse. I'm not sure I could have functioned at all without it. On the other hand, I had no clue how much harder it would be later. I had this false sense that I would get through this quickly. What an optimist!

I know he's not coming back. But I still catch myself thinking, "What if . . . ?". Tonight, I had this crazy thought that, maybe if I had just gone out to look for him again, I would have found him alive. I've mentioned before that the brain can play cruel tricks on you. For a split second, I actually thought that maybe I did it wrong. Perhaps I just didn't find him?! Why would I even think that?

I often wonder if I am "doing grief wrong." I'm becoming more aware of my tendency to stuff all the feelings inside me, which has been an excellent strategy so far, but I probably need to start letting it out a little more.

Okay, enough sadness! Yesterday, Matt was going through beer stuff, since there were many ingredients in the fridge and I don't make or drink beer. I have decided that Patrick would want me to ensure beer is always in his fridge. Denny and Matt have agreed to keep beer on tap at my house, and I think that's cool. Patrick would be pleased that people were still coming by for a glass of beer! While he was here, Matt figured out the keg in the fridge still had a bit of Patrick's second-to-last batch of beer. He decided to try it and pronounced it "Really, really, really good!" We laughed about it because there was no way Patrick would have ever let beer age for seven months. And it turns out that it does get better over time! I knew we would probably keep finding surprises, and I hope there are more left to discover.

ENTRY 39

L ife is unfair. Sometimes, bad things happen to good people. These are inadequate things to say when someone has died tragically. But most of us are at a loss for words when the unexplainable happens. My best friend Cathy's dad walked across the street Saturday night to get the mail. On his way back across, he was hit and killed. Why? Why? Why?

I met Cathy Stebles in fifth grade. Over the years, I got to know her entire family. Her parents, Ron and Charlene, were like second parents to me. I spent a lot of time at their house on East Herndon. Ron was one of a kind. He had a really dry sense of humor, and he always had us laughing. He had his own unique expressions. During high school, he would ask us if we had "met any lumps lately?" He was referring to hunks, but needed to make up his own word for it.

He raised his three daughters and one son to be independent. They learned to drive tractors before cars, and had to be able to change the oil and tires on their vehicles if they expected to be allowed to drive. A lot of his little quirks were brilliant. If he were driving us somewhere, he would buckle his seat belt and say, "One." Everyone knew this was their queue to count off as they buckled their seat belts. "Two, three, four," we all recited. This way, he knew all the kids were in the car and safely buckled in. He and Charlene always referred to me as one of their other kids.

Once we were adults, even though I didn't see them often, they were always very friendly and made me feel part of their family when I did.

Ron owned an auto shop called Speed Unlimited and mostly worked on Volkswagen vehicles. When Patrick bought his VW bus, he took it there for repairs and maintenance. When you own a 1971 VW bus, you know your mechanic well! Patrick and Ron had a similar sense of humor and enjoyed their frequent, brief visits. I also saw Ron often, since I spent time transporting Patrick from the shop to work and back again. I am grateful that I had these extra opportunities over the years.

I don't recall the exact dates Ron retired and sold the shop, but it was after we moved to Clovis. Ron introduced Patrick to Burnett's Auto Repair, and they worked on the bus for the rest of Patrick's life. When Patrick died, I was concerned about notifying them. The bus had been in the shop that week, and I wasn't sure they had seen news reports. Cathy talked to her dad, and he agreed to stop by and notify them. Ron and Charlene attended Patrick's funeral service. Seeing them was a bit of a shock to me, since I wasn't aware of Ron ever attending any kind of church service. I would describe Ron as a devout atheist. The fact that he sat through a Catholic funeral mass meant the world to me and made me realize how much he loved Patrick and me.

I saw Ron again at his grandson Matt's graduation. Matt graduated with my nephew, Anthony. Cathy had an extra seat, so I sat with the Stebles and Lamb family to free up a seat in the teNyenhuis section. I last saw Ron at the Cougar Foundation BBQ in September. As always, I received a big hug. He called me "Kiddo" and reminded me I was always "one of the kids." I'm grateful for these last few brief visits.

Me, Mike and Cathy Lamb, Michael Lamb, Ron and Charlene Stebles

And now my heart aches for his family, especially the grandkids. I know their pain only too well, and I wish they didn't have to endure this heartbreak. Ron lived a long, prosperous life. He was supposed to die years from now of old age. Some will say that at least he didn't suffer. It is even more senseless that someone his age would die tragically. The fact that it was one day short of seven months after Patrick died is unbelievable.

Cathy was my rock when Patrick died. I can never repay the support she gave me. Now our roles are reversed, but I'm not happy that I am returning the favor. It's not fair that she is going through this! I don't understand, but I know that I don't always get to know why things happen. I am hoping Patrick was able to welcome Ron with open arms. Ron would disagree, and I don't want to disrespect him, but I genuinely believe he is in heaven now. I just wish I could hear what he has to say about it. You know it would be good!

ENTRY 40

Yesterday was Thanksgiving and I've been watching everyone posting about everything they are thankful for. They are all very eloquent; some even mention an empty chair at the table. I wanted to write something cheery yesterday, since I genuinely have much to be thankful for. Yet I just couldn't bring myself to be grateful for anything. There is a hole in my heart that may get smaller someday, but it seems like it will always be there.

I know that Cathy's mom, Charlene, can relate, because Ron's sudden death was a tragedy similar to what I went through. Everyone who stopped by to see Charlene wanted to help, and most didn't know what to say. The most common thing people say in this situation seems to be, "What can I get you? Is there anything you need?" Charlene answered truthfully, "Yes, I need my husband. Can you get him?" My heart broke each time I heard her plea, because I remember having the same conversations. I may not have responded that way each time, but it was what I was thinking. Even though logically I knew it wasn't possible, having my husband back was the only thing I wanted too.

I intentionally planned something entirely different for this first Thanksgiving since Patrick died—to surround myself with almost 30 people most dear to me in one large, 10-bedroom inn. Any other option would have been so much worse. And yet, while I was truly grateful for us being together, I still wondered how I could make this holiday joyful with Patrick missing. I know he isn't missing, though. He is always nearby in our thoughts. He would have loved this trip, but it would have never happened if he had been here. There's no way he would have agreed to the expense.

Yesterday, we gathered in a circle to say grace. The family I was born into intermingled with the one I married into. My Dad, Kandra, Denise, Dawan, Tom, Denny and his girls, and Nick. Mom and Pop teNyenhuis; Gabe; Dom; Caitlin; Matt, Tina, and their kids; Sierra; Camille; and me. We asked Pop to say grace, and when he finished, Mom thanked me for bringing us all together. She said, "We are more complete when we are together." Then there were tears and lots of hugs. How lucky am I that my two families love each other so much? Later, we were joined by my nephew, Dustin, his girlfriend, Jenna, and Dina and Jeff. We've all been hanging out and enjoying each other's company.

I chose the Central Coast for this gathering because my family has spent many Thanksgivings at the North Beach campground. Since there were so many of us, we didn't join my extended family at the campground, but today we had a surprise party to celebrate my Aunt Emma's 80th birthday. They tricked her by telling her it was a surprise party for *my* birthday, so of course she ran out and bought me a card. After we ate, multiple family members got up to speak, and a few who had married into the family spoke of how much they appreciated being a part of our family. Everyone got choked up when they talked about Aunt Emma and the extended Boyles family. We also remembered my Uncle Joe, who passed away unexpectedly. Emma and Joe were married for over 50 years. She is now married to a friend of many years, Rex, who lost his wife after Uncle Joe died. A lighthearted moment was when my dad's former aunt spoke of how she loved the family so much that she married into it twice! Her husband was my grandma's brother, and he unfortunately passed away when they were driving back to Oklahoma after attending my sister's wedding. My uncle, her nephew by marriage, drove out to escort her back.

They were pretty close in age, and after several years of hanging around and helping her out, he married her. We joke about how Uncle Ed married his Aunt Vanda, but I assure you it was perfectly legal!

So I sat there listening to all the great memories and was reminded that I am genuinely thankful for my family. They are why I continue to get out of bed each day, and why I can continue moving forward. I'm frequently angry that I have to do it without Patrick, but I know he would love how much we all cherish our time together. We make more of an effort to be together now, and I get to have both of my families with me. I also look at Emma and Vanda, knowing they deeply loved their first husbands. They also lost their husbands suddenly, and they kept moving forward. I know I can do that too!

ENTRY 41

Today was a tough day for me. We had our second court appearance. I'm still not supposed to go into much detail about the case, although I wonder how much of a difference it would make since the potential sentence is already so small. Let me just say that the whole legal system is complex and sluggish. Nothing happens quickly, and there are always surprises. Each step of the way, something new comes up that affects how I feel, and right now, I don't even know how to think about the whole thing.

Since it is a misdemeanor case, it is in a busy courtroom with many other issues going on at the same time. They usually do our case first, probably since we have so many spectators. Many people around us are there for their cases, and I'm sure they want to clear us out of there to make room, which is fine. While waiting, I glance to my left, and a young lady gives me a warm smile and a nod. I later discover she is part of the defendant's family, maybe his wife. I'm unsure if she knew who I was, but I think she did. I choose to interpret the look as some sort of gesture of compassion.

I just feel there is no point in being here. Nothing happening here will bring Patrick back, and I just want to be somewhere else.

The other hard part is that I'm not the only one hurting. I was trying to keep my tears inside, but if I look around, I can see the pain in everyone else's faces. I hurt for me. I hurt for Patrick's siblings. My heart breaks for Barbara, who is sitting next to me, and for everyone else there. So much pain.

After the hearing, the DA takes us into the cafeteria to answer questions and discuss the next hearing date. As different family members speak, there are more tears. And suddenly, I realize this is what has become of my marriage. For 24 years, Patrick was the closest person to me. We shared everything that was happening in our lives. Decisions, plans, dreams. His life was mine. It's hard to say this, but it suddenly feels like our tight little circle is broken. I don't want to sound like I don't want others to care, or that anyone is upsetting me, but this whole situation kind of steals the intimacy of our relationship. I'm unsure if that makes sense, but it is how I feel today. And I just don't want to be here anymore.

Later in the day, I go to Camille's first soccer game of the season. I've been anticipating this for months. Last season was really exciting and will always be a special memory for me. The girls and their families have shown us so much love and support that I am thrilled to be around them again.

I also feel Patrick's absence. I want to share the excitement with him and keep imagining things he would say. And Camille is still having ankle issues. She is fine today, but her ankle is constantly swollen. Zio Matt is now her physical therapist; he has given her instructions and even checked in with her last night. But when I saw how swollen it was, I just wanted her dad to be here and be in charge of making it better. He took such good care of her; you can't duplicate that. She has coaches and trainers, but it's just not right that her dad is not here. She is able to play the entire game, though, and they win 4-0. So the outlook for the season is great!

ENTRY 42

LONELINESS – DECEMBER 4, 2016

One of the hardest things to deal with these days is loneliness. Not the "I'm alone and have no one to hang out with" kind. I miss having someone who loves me, knows everything about me, and loves me anyway. I miss having someone who will hold me if I need to cry. I miss having a husband. I miss *my* husband. Unfortunately, this is the kind of lonely that can't be filled right now.

I'm not interested in meeting someone new at this point, so let's not even start those discussions. I can love again, but I think I would be very, very picky. I was always grateful that I didn't have to experience much of the "dating" scene, and I still don't have any desire to do that. I'm thankful that I've connected with a lot of widows. Some are friends who lost their husbands before I did. Some are new friends, and some of those I have never even met in person. They "get" it.

The nice thing about knowing so many widows is that they are all at different points. Some have even married again. I feel hopeful when I see they have moved forward and can function. That's comforting. Some days, I wonder how I can even go on without Patrick. Seeing others who are moving forward gives me hope.

Every day, I am surprised that I still have such raw feelings. I can go for more extended periods feeling relatively okay, and I often feel happy. Still, I am randomly assaulted with vivid memories. They don't have to be anything significant.

Today, Matt came over to look at Camille's ankle and taught me how to massage it to relieve swelling. As I held her ankle and began massaging, she casually mentioned that Patrick had also massaged her ankle in this way. I imagined his hands massaging the same areas I was touching. It made me feel close to him, but I was also incredibly sad that he was not here to do it.

ENTRY 43

Yesterday, I started working on my afghan for the first time since Patrick died. I'm using an infinity loom, and technically, it is knitting, which I don't know how to do without the loom. I bought the loom when I was recuperating from surgery in early 2015. It took me the rest of that year to finish an afghan that I was making for Cathy. She's always cold, and the color I had chosen was one of her favorites. I finished her afghan on January 1 of this year, according to the date stamp of the picture I took. I started my own afghan right after that and, so far, I've done about four inches. So I have a long way to go.

I chose soft yarn that is multicolored with deep pinks and purples. I like the loom because you don't need to count each stitch. On Cathy's afghan, I alternated stitches and did an entire row at a time. For mine, I chose a basketweave pattern, and it's kind of a pain! Four knit stitches and then four purl stitches repeated throughout the row. You do three more rows precisely like that and then switch the order. You end up with little four-by-four squares of alternating stitches, and it is pretty. But it takes focus, and I haven't had much of that.

Eight months later, I now have no idea what row or stitch I was on. I remembered that I made notes to figure out which stitch sequence I was on, but I had no idea which row, and that's a problem with this pattern. After agonizing over it, I decided I would pick where I thought I was, and if it resulted in imperfection, so be it.

Maybe my afghan will be like the growth rings on a tree—showing nice and orderly growth, and then a shock to the system. For trees, this shock could be a fire or drought. For me, it was the upheaval of my life when Patrick died. I decided that, even if the work is imperfect, I would eventually return to a set pattern, and the afghan would remind me that I kept moving forward despite the shock to my system.

Everyone always tells me how strong I am, so I must be missing my calling. Clearly, I'm a good actress! The girls returned to their old routines relatively quickly, and I am still not working. Younger people are resilient, but I am still proud of their accomplishments! I try to be careful about what I write about them, but I will make an exception and be a proud Mama for a bit!

My girls each received communications from teachers this week that spoke to their ability to weather this tragedy, and not only function but excel in their schoolwork. Sierra's occurred when she turned in a final assignment. Camille's was via comments on letters of recommendation she received from several teachers. I also had a chance to read several essays Camille wrote for scholarship applications. Out of respect for their privacy, I will not share specific essays, letters, or comments, but I am proud of them!

Today, I am 49 years and 8 days old. This age is significant because Patrick was 49 years and 7 days old on the day he died. I used to joke that he would always be older than me, and now I have passed him up.

Strangely, I will continue aging, and he won't. I've said from the beginning that Patrick hated the thought of getting old. I imagine he's laughing a little at the idea of me passing him up, and if there's any solace, it's the fact that he doesn't have to experience old age or any of the physical problems that come with it. I, on the other hand, will continue making growth rings. I hope each year I cover up more of the scars from 2016. They'll never be gone entirely, but time will lessen their impact.

As I got ready to put away my afghan for the night, I remembered that I *did* have a way to track the rows. I had been using a row counter, and when I searched my bag, there it was! I was working on row 32 before April 20. This discovery conflicted with what I had determined, and I should have changed my pattern at the end of that row. Instead, I continued for two more rows, so now I will have four-by-six boxes instead of four-by-four. I could pull out the two rows and fix them, but I will leave it as it is. The imperfection will serve as a reminder that this was a bad year, but there will be other years.

I will grow stronger—never the same, but on the path to all the blessings I know I will experience in future years. Just like a fire can devastate a forest, 2016 has devastated me. This devastation will always be a part of my history, but I can make new, healthy growth rings, and that's what I choose to do.

ENTRY 44

STORIES WE TELL ON EACH OTHER – DECEMBER 20, 2016

Patrick died eight months ago today. I'm amazed I have made it eight months without him. Not that I had a choice. Sometimes, I feel like a broken record; I still can't believe he's gone! As we draw closer to Christmas, it gets harder and harder. I find myself incredibly sad when I least expect it. And I'm a little angry right now because this was not how things were supposed to go. I believe God has a plan, even if I don't understand it. I just wish that we could follow my plan. My plan was much better; it included joyfully watching our daughters achieve their dreams, having their father walk them down the aisle, and watching his joy as he held his first grandbaby. I need to find a way to enjoy those moments for both of us.

On Monday, I received a Christmas card from someone I don't know. The card was from one of Patrick's patients. She indicated he had treated her in 2007 and 2009. She told me he was an excellent PT, and the girls and I were his world. She also shared a funny story he had told her about me. I will never live this one down!

When the girls were in elementary school, I was sick one day. I didn't feel like getting out of bed, but I had to take them to school. So I just got in the car with my pajamas on. They were blue with large clocks on them for some reason. They were goofy-looking but soft and warm. Patrick liked to make fun of them. I drove the girls to school and dropped them off. I headed home, traveling south, and was at the stop sign closest to my house (it's now a traffic signal). A teenage boy was traveling east in the left turn lane. He started turning left, and I pulled into the intersection. But he wasn't turning left. He was making a U-turn, and I ran right into him! I was so annoyed. I just wanted to get back home and crawl into bed. Flustered, I put my van into reverse to exit the intersection and backed right into the car behind me! I was *so* embarrassed. I pulled over and sat in my van until the kid walked over, and I gave him my info.

Fortunately, the guy behind me surveyed his vehicle and decided he had no damage, so he left. The moral of the story is: Don't Leave Your House in Your Pajamas!

I think it's funny he told her that story. I told it to my coworkers too. I have no problem laughing at myself, and Patrick didn't mind laughing at himself for the most part. He's been gone eight months, and strangers are still reaching out to share his impact on them and their impressions of how he valued us, his family. I love hearing the stories, and it makes me want to reach out to people who have impacted me. Maybe that would be a good New Year's resolution.

Patrick was occasionally sensitive about stories that he felt were particularly embarrassing. However, he also liked to say, "It's only funny until someone gets hurt. Then it's hilarious!" And frankly, I would love to annoy him enough that he would haunt me because I really miss him. So here goes . . .

On a trip to Vegas, possibly for Denny's 21st birthday, we were in the Tropicana with my sister, Denise, and brother-in-law, Wes. Patrick decided to try oysters on the half shell. I think Wes might have challenged him or something. I guess you're supposed to just swallow them whole. So Patrick started making an exaggerated face like he was having trouble swallowing the oyster. We were all laughing at the faces he was making. Apparently, he wasn't trying to be funny, because suddenly the oyster came back up and flew across the table. We were dying laughing! We all had to walk away!

After that, it became a favorite topic whenever we were around Wes. Patrick eventually asked if we could put the story to rest, and I respected that while he was alive. Now I need reasons to laugh and smile, so I think he would understand!

ENTRY 45

There was another hearing today, and there will be another one in February. It's tough being there since nothing that happens will change the fact that Patrick is gone. Since the charge is a misdemeanor, all the hearings are in a misdemeanor courtroom, unlike what you see on TV. Many misdemeanor charges only require one court appearance, and the time spent there is brief. So, at any given time, many people are sitting around waiting for their case to be called. We walk in and usually take up almost a third of the seats. People line up before the doors open, and then they typically sit in the middle of the row, so you have to climb over them. It's very impersonal and offensive that Patrick's case doesn't warrant its own courtroom.

Another difference from TV is that there is no special section for the families of the defendant and the victim. And since there are only three rows, you might end up next to the defendant's family or behind them, like I was today. On the way out, one of them spoke to me. I think she was his aunt or possibly his grandmother. My brain gets a little foggy at times like this. She told me she was sorry, it was an accident, and she was praying for us. Her words were not well-received by anyone in my family. We are all dealing with various degrees of pain and anger, and everyone is very protective of me. I chose to believe that she was telling me that her nephew (grandson?) did not intentionally set out to kill Patrick. I never thought he did, but I believe his choices led to

Patrick's death. I felt it was brave and kind of her to speak to me. I would have felt compelled to say something if I were in the same position.

Today, the defendant appeared almost happy, which was also upsetting to many. However, he had four family members there, and I suspect at least one was his child. I have to think that was what made him happy. Unfortunately, the penalty options are limited, so there is no part of this that is going to make everyone in my family happy. We just need to try to get through it.

I often wonder what Patrick would think or feel about all of this. His priority would be to shield us from pain as much as possible. I always keep that in mind. I always sense that whatever I do, whatever decisions I make, it is okay. I don't need to agonize; I still have his love and support. However I act or feel is the right way. I think he would want to ensure this didn't happen to anyone else, but at the end of the day, his family would be his priority.

As we left court today, a flock of birds flew by. I think there were at least two ostriches or pterodactyls because they left two humongous sprays of bird poop on my new car! The crap all over the window summed up how we all felt. We had a good laugh and, after dropping everyone off, I immediately went through a car wash. Life will send a lot of crap our way, and it's not always pleasant. I choose to let it wash away. I won't forget it, but I don't have to carry it around. I don't mean to oversimplify grief, but I think you must get through however you can. Embrace the positive and let the pain wash away as much as possible.

ENTRY 46

A few days ago, I was driving home from an appointment, enjoying my new car's heated seats and stereo. I was thinking of how much I love my new gym and feeling unusually happy. Inevitably, when this happens, I feel guilty because I probably wouldn't be enjoying any of these things if Patrick was still here.

Getting used to living without your spouse is really hard. First, there is the actual living: waking up, getting out of bed, getting dressed, eating. None of those things were easy at first. I went through the motions and, eventually, it got a little easier. Once you master continuing to be alive, you have to decide if you will ever really *live* again. That is a little harder to come to terms with.

A lot has changed for me, and not all of it is awful. I am in school, learning new things. I am recently taking better care of myself. I am cooking and kind of enjoying it a little. I am keeping my house tidy so that someone else can clean it deeply! I've learned to do more around the house and yard. I have a lot of new friends and deeper relationships with older friends. I get paid to be retired! My retirement future is more secure than it would have been. I will get to enjoy my retirement years.

My life is pretty okay right now, and it sucks that Patrick is not here to enjoy it with me. The thing is, as much as losing him sucks, it happened. It's my reality. It makes no sense that God would take him from the girls and me, but we don't always get to know the reason. And even though most of my new life would have never been had Patrick lived, it IS. I like to say, "It is what it is." This is the life I have been given. I can choose to spend all of my time mourning, or I can choose to live.

I decided to look up the meaning of "It is what it is." The definition I found in the Urban Dictionary is kind of harsh and uses multiple curse words, but does sum things up perfectly. This is the way it's going to be! Deal with it! I am going to try and enjoy things without guilt. I know this is what Patrick would've wanted.

I won't apologize for knowing my new friends or enjoying my car. My happiness doesn't mean that I don't miss him. I will always think about him. Every. Single. Day. Hopefully, it will be with a smile on my face.

Earlier, I was sitting at Camille's soccer game. As is typical, we weren't happy with some of the calls, and the other coach was a little obnoxious. One of the dads was being quite vocal about it, and his wife scolded him a little. I laughed to myself and thought this was the first time I was happy Patrick was not there. He probably would have considered it a challenge to be more obnoxious, and I would have worried that he would get the ref angry. I would have said "PATRICK!!!!!!!" many times! I would have said his name quickly and quietly because he didn't like me to scold him. And *maybe* he would have listened, or probably he would have just gotten up and walked away. I guess I would have been happy to deal with him if he could have been there. Instead, I just laughed and smiled. It doesn't always hurt unbearably, and it's good when I have a happy or funny memory.

I will keep working on the guilt. It is a work in progress, and that's fine.

ENTRY 47

This week is going to be difficult for me. We have a court appearance on Thursday, and I believe there will be sentencing. We are supposed to be prepared to speak if we choose to. I wrote a statement months ago, and I probably won't change it much, but I will agonize until it is time to read it. What do you say to the man who hit and killed your husband and the father of your children? I feel like I need to be mean and angry, but I am truly not capable of doing that. I have asked my brother to speak also. He is an eloquent writer and speaker, and he will be able to convey anger better than I can. I will still speak because he needs to know what he took away from us. Speaking won't be easy, but it will be good when it is behind us.

Yesterday, I spoke with George Drysdale, the physical therapist who happened to be one of the first people on the scene. I spoke with him in April and meant to contact him again when I had more time. I was very comforted speaking with him. George told me he got there moments after the car hit Patrick and it was still dark. He saw cars parked along the right side of the road. He could barely see people standing around and someone was motioning for him to pull off the road. George said, "I stepped out of the truck to assess the situation and I noticed a man sitting on the ground with his head in his hands, looking confused." George looked around and saw a car in a gully and then noticed another man who lay on the ground with a bike.

George confirmed that another bystander was on the phone with 911. George went over to the man, who he later learned was Patrick, and determined there was no pulse. George said, "I had full intention to lay my hands on him and pray over him to bring him back to us, back to his broken body. But somehow I knew that strong, healthy man on the ground was gone. He was by God's side." George told me his recollection was that the driver was very distraught and appeared confused and worried. The driver told them that Patrick had swerved in front of him and suddenly he was flying over the car. George and the others could see that the driver's car had left the road, so they were confused by the driver's explanation. George said, "We were all in shock and, together with the driver, we prayed over Patrick." After praying, with the 911 operator still on the phone, George and another bystander attempted CPR until paramedics arrived. Even though they knew it was futile, George wanted to feel he had done what he could.

George said, "Performing CPR, something I've had to do before, was more of an act of duty in my heart than a lifesaving effort."

This experience profoundly affected George, and he was grateful to talk to me and answer any questions he could. George is a cyclist and frequently rides the route Patrick was on, so he immediately felt a connection. He felt even more connected when he learned Patrick was a fellow physical therapist.

George felt somewhat guilty that he was not able to do anything and has struggled with questioning whether he should have started CPR sooner. I reassured him that I knew there was nothing he could have done. I didn't think of this when I spoke to him, but it just occurred to me that maybe God put him there so I would know there were loving people who prayed over Patrick and could tell me he appeared at peace. Having George there meant so much to me! The first time we met, at Patrick's rosary, he told me he and his wife had been praying for the girls and me, and she wanted me to know she was sending her love. I spoke to her for the first time last night, and she is kind and loving. I'm adding them to the list of my new forever friends.

I hadn't thought much about the other people there, and I have no idea who they were. Maybe someday I will be put in contact with them, and I can thank them for stopping.

ENTRY 48

It is said that at the end of your life, memories flash before you. I didn't realize that when you lose someone who was such a big part of your life, this video montage seems to go on and on. At times, it's jarring when I suddenly remember some random event. Cathy and I drove to Las Vegas this week to see Cher in concert. As we passed the casinos in Primm, I looked at the big roller coaster that I'm pretty sure I had never ridden, but suddenly, I remembered riding roller coasters with Patrick. It's almost like an alarm your body sets if you go too long without thinking about your loved one. Some of these memories almost bring me to tears, but I'm trying to learn to smile and let the memory fill my heart.

Recently, I remembered the beautiful box my mother-in-law made for us to put cards in at the wedding. The idea was to have one place to keep all the cards so they wouldn't get lost, and it was a great idea! We gathered at my mom's house the morning after the wedding to open gifts. Someone mentioned the cards at some point, and no one could find the box. Patrick and I were anxious to get going, so we left without looking for the box. We drove to San Francisco and flew to Puerto Rico, where we left on a seven-day cruise.

While we began our honeymoon, our families were trying to solve the mystery of the card box. The box had been placed on the roof of a van while a child was being buckled into a car seat in the garage of our new apartment. The box fell off somewhere between that apartment complex and my mom's house. Family members walked most or maybe all of the route in a fruitless search for the box.

We called to check in a few days later and, at that point, our families had taken on the awkward task of determining what had been in the box. Some guests had written checks that could be canceled and rewritten. Some had given us gift cards or cash, so those were lost. A few weeks later, a friend was in a meat market where he had purchased a gift certificate for us. His friends owned the meat market, and he was visiting them when someone came in and tried to redeem the gift certificate. The owners got it back, but didn't get any info on the person. From that point on, we knew that the box had been found and someone chose to keep our cards and the gifts inside them.

At first, I was sad, and then we felt victimized. I just couldn't believe someone would be so coldhearted. The relative who had placed the box on the van's roof felt terrible and sent us a new TV as a gift. We wanted to send it back, since it wasn't his fault. But we were finally convinced that he would not feel better unless we accepted it.

As the years went by, the impact of this seemed smaller and smaller. The loss of the card box would not ruin our memories of a fabulous time in our lives. Sure, we thought about what we could have done with the money, but eventually, it became a distant memory.

I share this as a reminder that sometimes we go through situations that seem like the end of the world, but eventually, those memories soften with time, and you realize they were just a tiny blip. Just to clarify, I am *not* comparing the loss of the cards to the loss of Patrick. Losing Patrick will always have a significant impact on me. My main point is, "Don't let bad experiences define you." This experience taught me that what matters is love and family.

You can have all the money in the world, but I would rather have the people I love. When I reflect on my wedding, the card box is a small part of the memories, and the rest are *joyous*!

Our wedding day, June 27, 1992

ENTRY 49

I've stayed busy all week so I don't think about tomorrow. We have our final hearing, and we will be addressing the defendant. I have been anxiously awaiting this closure. It didn't happen two weeks ago, but I am 99 percent sure this will be it. I've been keeping my guard up, and I will probably have to let it down tomorrow, which terrifies me. My family will be with me, so I know it will be okay. But I'm not sure I want to experience all the emotions. At least this part will be over.

ENTRY 50

CLOSURE – FEBRUARY 20, 2017

The court case is finally over. The defendant will spend 316 days in a treatment facility. We had the opportunity to read our statements (I have included them in the Appendix). The defendant either chose not to face us, or was not allowed to, so we read our statements to his back.

Today marks 10 months since Patrick's death. I can't believe it's been that long, yet it seems like yesterday. There have been so many ups and downs since then, and so many more to come. I made it through two difficult days last week, and I think I only have a few more "firsts" left: Saint Patrick's Day, Easter, his birthday, and the first anniversary of his death a week later. I'm sure the second year won't be much easier, but at least I will be past all the firsts.

Since we have had our final court date, I will share more about that.

My understanding is that, several days before the incident, the man who hit Patrick had argued with his wife and left with their car. For three days and nights, he used the car as an illegal or "ghetto" taxi (his words). He explained that people knew he had a car and would call him for rides. He admitted to smoking meth during this time, and there was meth found in his blood. His phone records revealed very few periods with no activity, so he was more than likely sleep-deprived. He said he was driving out Shaw Avenue to return a backpack to someone who had left it in his car. Coincidentally, there was a meth pipe in the bag. He said

Patrick just veered in front of him. I'm sure he wanted to believe that, but the evidence did not support that. The detective investigated extensively and determined that the driver left the road and hit Patrick. We assume that he fell asleep.

At the scene, he was distraught and failed the first sobriety test. They administered a second one a little later, and the second officer advised him to "get it together," and he passed. The conflicting results were the first issue that made the case difficult. When they found meth in his system, we all thought it would be a felony. The problem is that drug intoxication is much more challenging to measure. In California, it's against the law to drive while impaired by drugs, but there is no clear definition of impairment. An ER doctor who has testified as an expert witness was consulted during the investigation and indicated he could just as easily testify for the defense, which effectively ended the pursuit of felony charges.

I plan to spend a lot of time learning more about drug impairment and distracted driving, but I also want to know about punishment and deterrents. What can be done to prevent this type of offense? I realize there won't be a quick or simple answer, but I appear to have lots of time, since most of my future plans were destroyed.

Thursday was the most time we had to spend in the courtroom. I'm still unsure why, but it took over two hours before they brought the defendant in. When he finally arrived, we started pretty quickly, and the whole hearing lasted no more than 15 to 20 minutes. At the end of my statement, I held up the picture of Patrick and the girls that is currently my Facebook profile picture, and then I played Patrick's recording of "Blackbird." I told the court that I felt it was a love letter to the girls and me, and it could also be a message to the defendant: "Take these broken wings and learn to fly." At the very least, I thought he should hear Patrick's voice, so I was glad I had that to play.

Speaking was harder than I thought. I cried throughout and sobbed when I sat back down. The worst part was that I knew it was hard for my family to see and hear. The girls did not attend court, but I had my mom, my dad, my step-mom, my mother-in-law, all three of my siblings, my brother-in-law, two of my sisters-in-law, two of my nieces, and three cousins. Plus, a news reporter who happens to be a friend. When it was over, we left the courtroom, and I said quick goodbyes and headed to Bakersfield to watch Camille's team win round two of the playoffs! I'll admit that I asked Patrick to put in a good word with the man upstairs for favorable weather and a win.

I am happy to have court behind me, but it's a very odd feeling—kind of a reverse letdown. I guess I thought it would be more of a relief. But in the end, Patrick is still gone. I put a lot of energy and emotion into getting through court, and I thought I would feel an enormous weight lifted. The problem is that none of it changes anything. We knew it would never provide justice or peace, but I was still hoping that I might feel closure.

So now I need to continue moving forward and try to find joy. It's not going to be easy, but I've got to try—for my girls, for Patrick, and for me.

ENTRY 51

It's after midnight on March 17, and Camille is still working on homework. I have made sure I am wearing green because we take that very seriously in our house. Patrick loved seeing who wasn't wearing green and ensuring they were pinched. It was a silly tradition, but we always had fun with it. I always thought it was cool that my husband had a special day for his name.

The kids next door loved Patrick. Last year on March 17, I went out to get the mail and ran into our neighbor, Brandie. She told me her son, Evan, a first grader, couldn't wait for Patrick to get home so he could wish him a happy birthday! She tried to explain that it wasn't his birthday, but he wasn't buying it. I watched for Patrick to get home, and Evan quickly ran over when he did. Patrick told him he was crazy or something and then acted crazy with a silly voice. I used to worry that his behavior would scare kids, since he would yell things like, "What are you doing on my sidewalk?!" Kids always seemed to "get" him, though. As he ranted at them, Evan and his little sister, Tabitha, would giggle. I always got a kick out of watching him with them.

Recently, it occurred to me that Evan and Tabitha might not remember Patrick anymore, and the thought made me sad. Then I spoke to Brandie right after the last hearing, and she told me she had seen a news report about the case that included a video of me speaking (breaking down) at the sentencing. She said she cried, and Evan cried, which was even sadder.

When someone is gone, you seem to remember them with rose-colored glasses. My Patrick wasn't really a saint, but he was a good man, and a lot of people loved him. As hard as it is to miss him every day, it's a blessing to know how many people he positively impacted (even if it was just making them laugh). People still share stories about Patrick with me, and I always enjoy hearing them. My greatest wish is to keep his memory alive and to live life doing things that would make him proud or just make him laugh.

ENTRY 52

I would like to start by apologizing to my children. I try not to embarrass them, but sometimes I must be a mom! Patrick and I have always been proud of the girls. One of the things I miss the most is our private conversations about our hopes and dreams for them. We could just talk and not worry if we sounded like we were bragging. We thought we were the luckiest people in the world! We joked that we were terrible parents, and I frequently thought we might have been too easy on them. Mainly, we just loved and enjoyed them.

One thing I regret is that I don't have a lot of videos of them interacting with their dad. They all regularly entertained me. When they were younger and video cameras were popular, I wanted to enjoy life, not walk around recording it. But I would love to have just a few videos of the crazy arguments and discussions they had!

The girls have been remarkably strong and resilient in their own ways. Sierra took incompletes in her college classes last spring. She is finishing those up and will graduate after three years of college. Patrick and I had thought she was joking when she first told us of this plan, but she stuck with it and did exceptionally well. She had planned to go straight to law school, but will take a year to study for the Law School Admission Test (LSAT) to get into a good school. I am grateful that I don't have to be an empty nester yet.

Camille is graduating with just about every honor available. She is currently weighing her options, but has several good scholarship opportunities.

This week, there was an unfortunate event at Clovis East. Two students fought, and one cut or stabbed the other. Later that day, Camille and her friends were sad to see people commenting negatively on social media about their school. They decided to share the positives, and Camille began a tweet thread of positive things at the school this year. Others joined, and her tweets were shared hundreds of times. She didn't think she did anything special and was surprised at the response. She was not happy when she got a request for an interview from a local news station. She didn't want to do it, and when I asked her why, she said, "I'm really more of a behind-the-scenes person." She did the interview, though, and I thought she did great.

I'm very relieved that my daughters are strong and successful in life. They are both on the right track, and I'm excited to see what they accomplish. I am so blessed to be their mother!

ENTRY 53

I grew up with a seemingly endless crowd of pets and farm animals. We had pigs, goats, ducks, geese, cats, cows, rabbits, dogs, and a horse. I enjoyed having so many different animals, but I also knew they were a lot of work.

Patrick also grew up with pets, although his family didn't have as many.

When we were first married, Patrick had no desire to have a pet, and I was okay with that. After the girls were born and we moved to Clovis, we began discussing it. Patrick considered it one of those obligatory things that "good" parents do. Finally, he decided we could get a pet, but there were conditions. He got to pick the breed and the name. I was very nervous!

When he told me he wanted a pug, I was reluctant. They're kind of ugly with their flattened noses. He went to pick one out, and when he showed me the picture, I fell in love! Now he needed a name.

Patrick holding Aggie

One of my favorite movies is *The Birdcage* with Robin Williams and Nathan Lane. Hank Azaria plays a gay male maid who is hilarious. The maid's name is Agador Spartacus, and that is the name Patrick chose. I wasn't thrilled with his choice, but I did want a dog, so I agreed. The day "Aggie" came home, I left work early and picked him up. We had a plan to surprise the girls, so I waited with Aggie in the family room. When they walked in, Aggie was exploring the space. There was initial confusion and then shouts of glee when the girls realized that the adorable little black dog was theirs!

Aggie lived up to his crazy name. He had more personality than any dog I've ever known. He regularly entertained us with his goofy behavior. Patrick once asked me if I thought other people sat around and laughed at their dog. I wasn't sure about everyone else, but we did that frequently. He had crazy mannerisms and seemed to enjoy spinning, especially as Patrick ran the lawnmower.

Since we had a pool, we decided we needed to know if he could swim. He would paddle his paws before hitting the water and head immediately to the steps. He hated swimming, but would run back and forth, barking until you splashed him.

Patrick and I always thought it was ridiculous when people spent thousands of dollars on medical care for their pets. We would *never* do that! That changed on Father's Day one year when a bee stung Aggie. Patrick and the girls rushed him to the pet ER while I stayed with our guests. He spent four days there, but amazingly survived and lived many years after that. The pet ER sent us home with a cool reusable bag, other souvenirs, and a $2,000 bill. That was the best $2,000 we ever spent!

No strangers ever came to visit Aggie. Every person who came over was a special guest who was there to give him attention. He made sure you knew this, and rewarded you with as many licks as you would allow. If you were bald, like Uncle Denny, he would be happy to clean your head if it was within reach.

He was hyper when he was young but became calmer as he aged. At night, when he was tired, he would run upstairs to Camille's room (where he slept) and return with his stuffed chicken. Patrick would say, "Chicken time!" and we would all laugh. He really was part of the family!

After Patrick died, I expected to see Aggie looking for him. He never did. He still spent his nights with Camille, but during the day, he became my constant companion and stayed as close to me as possible. More than once, I thought I was going to trip over him. And I had to splash water on him to get him to move away from the tub so I could get out.

He got sick quickly, and within a few weeks, he started getting weak. This Friday, he could no longer stand on his back legs, although he seemed comfortable. He slowly deteriorated, and we knew it was time to let him go. We loved on him all weekend and took him to the vet today. We all cried but have been through worse, so we will get through this too.

Over the last 11 months, I often thanked Patrick for picking out
this incredible bundle of love. He brought a lot of cheer to our
lives during some of the darkest days. I like to think that when he
died he ran right into Patrick's arms, was scooped up, and told
what a good boy he was for taking care of us all this time. He was
the best! Rest in peace, my sweet little boy!

More Aggie photos

ENTRY 54

SURROUNDED BY LOVE – APRIL 21, 2017

I look at the "On This Day" feature on Facebook daily. Since Patrick was opposed to social media, he wasn't on there a lot, but I occasionally mentioned him in posts or snuck in a picture, and I'm always happy when they pop up as a memory.

As the first anniversary of his death has approached, I've known I would begin to have a considerable amount of posts in my feed starting on the 20th. Looking through them, I frequently said, "I am surrounded by love." I said these words repeatedly, because it was and is *so* true!

That love and the security it brought me has gotten me through the first year. There is a lot of discussion about what to say and do when someone experiences a loss. SURROUND THEM WITH LOVE!

Let me share some ways people reached out and surrounded us with love. Many people came to our house on the day of the crash and were physically there for us. Others called or texted. Paper plates, utensils, paper towels, and toilet paper showed up in mass quantities. People knew how large our families were and that we would need to be together, and they made that easier. Dishes were done, trash was taken out, leaves were skimmed out of the pool, and I didn't have to take care of anything for at least the first week, and really much longer.

Patrick's uncle and aunt, Jim and Ineke Wood, their son, Jim Jr., and grandson, Elijah, did my yard for most of the first year. Denny and Matt helped often. Dawn Kuhl started a meal train, and friends and acquaintances brought food for two to three weeks. Linda Crews did laundry whenever I needed it. Cathy Lamb did whatever I needed.

Many people sent plants and flowers. Other people sent cards. For weeks, getting the mail gave me a sense of normalcy. Sometimes it was the only thing I did myself. I received a steady stream of cards and letters. I loved getting those, and I will try to be better about sending cards to people who have lost a loved one in the future.

Teachers at Clovis East collected gift cards to various fast-food places, which immensely helped. Others included gift cards or money in their cards. Granville Homes employees collected donations for my sister-in-law, Lisa, to give us, including $500 in Visa gift cards from one of the owners! I never realized funeral homes and cemeteries expect payment before the service. And it takes much longer for insurance policies to pay. I have a new appreciation for the car washes and GoFundMe drives for funeral expenses. I was fortunate to have Patrick's parents help with funeral expenses, and I didn't have to figure out how to pay. Not everyone has that kind of security. At first I felt guilty about getting cash gifts, but I appreciated them while I waited for other money. All of these gifts helped out a lot!

We got a lot of really thoughtful personal gifts too. Dawn, Tony, Logan, and Tylar gave us meaningful bracelets. My friend, Denise Hert, sent me a personalized necklace that said, "A piece of my heart lives in heaven" with Patrick's name, date of death, and an angel wing. I now wear it frequently.

My sister, Dawan, was in Europe when Patrick died. She gave me a crucifix from Notre Dame that was my constant companion for the first few weeks, and I held it when I addressed the defendant in court. Dawan also gave the girls and me necklaces.

One of Patrick's patients gave me a special poem and a wind chime that makes me think of Patrick when I hear it. The teNyenhuis aunts gave us a framed family picture.

Another really special gift came from Lucia Prandini's coworkers. Lucia's dad, Zio Angelo, died the day after Patrick. Her coworkers in Porterville gave Lucia, Zia (Aunt) Becky, and Angelino (Lucia's brother) each a cross wall hanging, and they gave us one also. Even though none of them knew us, they knew our story and what we were all going through.

People helped with the service. Lisa Boyles set up the memorial website for me. Jill Holstein and Mark Dorman made a beautiful tribute video. If I needed anything, people did it!

The girls each received special gifts from friends, and Camille's friends helped with the picture display boards.

There are many ways to help, and sometimes the biggest help is just being physically present or sharing thoughts and memories. I received countless texts and Facebook messages or posts. These words meant the world to me.

While looking through the posts from last year, I decided to edit my Facebook profile. I'd taken out the "happily married mother of two" wording a while back, but couldn't bring myself to change my relationship status from married to widowed. I didn't want it to be like I was advertising my status. I decided to check the profiles of a few other widows I know, and what I found broke my heart. A few didn't list a relationship status, and a few said they were still married. A lot said married to . . . with a link to the husband's profile. I'll admit I wished Patrick was on Facebook so I could put him on my relationship status. I know that is silly, since neither of us needed an affirmation of love. But I was always proud to be his wife, so I was bummed he wasn't on Facebook.

I can't imagine how much more challenging it would be for widows who must delete their relationship to change their status.

Suddenly, I was glad Patrick wasn't on Facebook. And yes, it did occur to me that maybe I shouldn't point out the relationship status to my widowed friends. I laughed as soon as I thought this because, of course, they know that they are no longer married. I'm sure they have also spent time deciding how to handle their status.

I changed my status to widowed. I wondered if I would ever change it again.

ENTRY 55

CHERISH – MAY 11, 2017

The other night, I was at the Clovis East Scholarship Awards for Camille. When the ceremony began, the couple sitting in front of me, friends of mine, reached out and grasped hands. A year ago, seeing this sign of affection would have made me incredibly jealous. I would be lying if I said it doesn't make me jealous now. But mostly, it makes me happy.

I've spent much time on the "appreciate your spouse" bandwagon, so I love seeing people doing just that! I've told my daughters that I want them to find someone to cherish them.

"Cherish" means *to protect and care for (someone) lovingly.* I especially like the word cherish because it makes me think of how Patrick cared for the girls and me. Anytime I drove somewhere without him, he would tell me to "drive safe" because I was "precious cargo." When we became parents, he expanded the definition of precious cargo to include the girls. I also used the word cherish to explain to one of my daughters that I hoped she would find a man who would cherish her, because she deserved nothing less.

Patrick cherished me and I cherished him. Our marriage wasn't perfect. Most marriages are not fairy tales. I think a good marriage is actually very unglamorous. I know I was so comfortable in my marriage that I didn't worry if I woke up with my hair looking like a rat's nest. I don't think I am an expert on marriage either.

I just know I was happy, and I can tell you what that looked and felt like.

We were kind to each other. We didn't belittle each other; if we had a problem, we would work it out. We respected each other. We gave each other space when needed. We listened and comforted each other. Patrick was my sounding board, and I was his. Yes, we sometimes annoyed each other, but the good outweighed the minor annoyances.

I cursed at Patrick exactly one time, and it upset him so much that I never did it again! We had gone skiing, and it was probably my second time ever. Dawan rode up the chair lift with me and was patiently helping me. When Patrick got off the lift, we had only gone around 50 feet, so he came over to see what the hold-up was. The hold-up was that Danell was a lousy skier! I fell every few yards (or was it feet or inches?). Patrick assessed the situation and made a true Patrick observation: "If you're going to fall, you probably should avoid the big drifts of snow since they are hard to get up from." As if I was strategically planning my falls! I simply said, "F$&@ you." He was stunned. Dawan looked at him and said calmly, "Maybe it would be better if we met you at the bottom?" He liked to remind me of that any time I was annoyed with him.

Do me a favor; just humor me. The next time you are annoyed with someone you love, take a deep breath and imagine how annoyed you would be if they were gone! Send them to the bottom of the hill for a break if needed. I know it's not always fun and games, but try to appreciate them as often as possible, because time is precious, and so are relationships.

ENTRY 56

TAKE THESE BROKEN WINGS – MAY 24, 2017

I still remember finding the recording of "Blackbird" on the day Patrick died. I believe it was a love song for the girls and me. The whole family has embraced this gift, and it's very special to us. I realize the song is about the civil rights movement, but for us, it has always meant that Patrick wanted us to "learn to fly" again.

At first, that was hard to imagine. I still have vivid memories of telling Sierra over the phone that her dad had died. When your world falls apart, you want those you love the most to be near you. It was agonizing to have her be four hours away, and I thank God Denise was living in Southern California then. I honestly don't know what we would have done if she hadn't been living there.

My girls were the only reason I was able to keep moving forward. As hard as it was for me, I couldn't imagine how it felt for them to lose their father at 17 or 19.

The Child Bereavement Estimation Model (CBEM) states that approximately 1 in 14 children under 18 will lose 1 parent before their 18th birthday. Roughly 25 percent of these children will experience mental health problems.

I just wanted my girls to be okay.

The CBEM also notes that a caring community, positive role models, healthy coping skills, peer support, and encouraging educators are all protective factors for children who lose a parent.

The crash site was half a mile from the high school where Patrick's brother taught math, and where Camille was a junior. That school and Camille's friends provided the most protective factors, and our large family provided the rest. But I knew Sierra would have very few protective factors when she returned to Long Beach in the fall.

I worried about how we would survive without Patrick. When he died, there was no question that Sierra would not finish her semester in Long Beach. We couldn't have been that physically far apart at that point. For months before Patrick's death, she had been telling us that she was graduating at the end of her third year. We thought it was wishful thinking, but she assured us it was happening. We were both very proud of her! I assumed Patrick's death would delay her plans and I remember thinking she could lighten her load and take more time to graduate.

I tried not to push either of the girls. I wanted us all to move forward, but I prepared myself for their struggles the next school year. I needed to make sure that I gave them unconditional love and support.

Sierra takes after me in some ways and is more emotional. She and I cried together a lot, while Camille dealt with her grief on her own schedule. Camille is a lot like her father, and I knew she would continue on her path to graduate from high school as a valedictorian.

Sierra has always been a good student. She graduated from high school with a decent GPA and multiple advanced placement classes. I knew she would be successful in life, but the summer after Patrick died, I worried that her dad's death would be a setback in her college career. I wondered if she would be emotionally prepared to leave her younger sister and me to return to school in the fall. So I was a little surprised when she told me she had an important interview scheduled.

Sierra had participated in high school speech, debate, and mock trial competitions. She had made it to state finals in speech and attended nationals one year. Though she had begun to talk about attending law school, I wasn't taking her very seriously.

In Long Beach, she participated in mock trial competitions too. Before Patrick's death upended her semester, she had applied for the moot court team at Long Beach. She explained it was a little more prestigious than a mock trial and would be somewhat time-consuming. The interview she had scheduled was for this team.

I was nervous. Would she be able to finish her makeup work, her fall semester, *and* do moot court? I would have been okay with her taking a semester off, but she wanted to move forward.

The team selected Sierra. Over the summer, we all went to grief counseling. I let them stop when they felt ready, which was sooner than when I stopped. In August, we moved Sierra back to Long Beach and said goodbye. This farewell was much more complicated than when she started college two years earlier. Now she had just one parent. I hoped that I would be enough support.

The team was a good experience. I believe it helped give Sierra some of the community and peer support she needed. I know that it boosted her confidence.

Returning to Long Beach in the fall was very hard for Sierra. She reminded me of her three-year goal and her goal of going to law school. I told her no one expected her to stick with that now. How could we? She was adamant about graduating, but finally conceded there was no shame in taking a year off between graduating and attending law school. She could have done the bare minimum and still graduated, and I would have been proud. She could have curled up in a ball and not left the house, and I would have understood. Instead, she went back and did *so* well that she completed all her makeup work with a 3.8 GPA for that semester. She did so well that she had three extra words added to her diploma, "Magna Cum Laude"! I don't know how she managed to do this. She had more strength and determination than I ever realized!

I am so proud she found her inner strength and finished school with honors! I know we still have challenging moments ahead of us, but it feels good to know that your child has faced adversity and beat it.

Sierra took the message to heart. She learned to fly instead of using her broken wings as an excuse. She thought about putting those words on her cap, but she didn't want to use the word "broken." I like what she chose: "All your life, you were only waiting for this moment to be free." It was a great tribute to Patrick.

Sierra

Of course, I shed a few tears the day she graduated. It was hard having that moment and not sharing it with Patrick. I know he is proud of her and always with us in spirit, but we all know it's not the same! So I had a lot of tears of sadness. I also had tears of joy and pride. Sierra faced adversity, and she rocked it! She will accomplish great things, and I am genuinely impressed by her!

Me and Sierra

ENTRY 57

I always knew Camille's high school graduation would be amazing! Each year, it became more apparent she would accomplish great things. From the time she started kindergarten, every teacher told us what a great student and all-around person she was. It was so exciting to watch her grow into the beautiful, intelligent young lady she is. We knew there would be honors; we just had no idea how many there would be. We couldn't wait for her senior year!

Experiencing her senior year without Patrick was so bittersweet. I always tried to remember he was with us in spirit, but that gets hard when you just want him physically present.

This has been a challenging year in many ways. I would have given both my girls a pass if they just phoned it in for the last year. That's all I expected. Instead, Camille discovered her strength and resilience like her big sister. Although she loved her dad deeply, she carried on exactly as he would have wanted. She radiated love, faith, and strength, and I believe it significantly impacted those around her.

She has kept the memory of her dad alive by recalling funny stories and always having a quick, hilarious response. Like her father, she is loving, but not overly emotional. She doesn't cry often, but wraps her arms around me if I need her to. And she never says goodbye without telling me she loves me. I knew Camille could be a leader, but she had always been shy. I knew that would be her biggest challenge. This year, she became a leader!

I don't know if you've seen the story about how we never know when we are experiencing the "lasts" with our kids: last bottle, last diaper, last time holding them, etc. Every time I read that story, I am amazed at how true it is! During the last few weeks before Camille graduated, I was asked to chaperone a field trip to the Asian Art Museum in San Francisco. It was fun to know that I was experiencing the last field trip!

During the museum tour, the students were put into groups, and they each had to find a particular exhibit, study it, and share it with the group. I was surprised that Camille was the spokesperson for her group! A few years ago, she would have sooner missed the field trip than speak in front of a group. She spoke in front of her classmates multiple times during her senior year and even managed to be poised and articulate when a TV station interviewed her.

I was overflowing with relief and joy! I was happy that Camille was coping and excelling. And, just for the record, she graduated second in her class as a valedictorian and an Academic Scholar of Distinction. She was also recognized as a life member of the California Scholastic Federation, received the Principal's Medallion, and was inducted into the National Honor Society! I can't wait to see her soar in college!

Sierra, Camille, and me

Camille had to miss Sierra's graduation due to senior events. Cathy surprised me by arranging for a photo shoot with both girls.

Camille and Sierra

ENTRY 58

I BOUGHT YOU A CAR! – JUNE 8, 2017

I don't burst into tears very often; if I do, it's usually when no one else is around. It snuck up on me today, and I almost cried at the smog check place. But I caught it and waited until I was in the car. And conveniently, I was right by the cemetery, so I went straight there.

I don't go there often. When I feel guilty, I remind myself that Patrick would flat-out tell me not to go there. I go when I feel the need to. I didn't stay long. Just long enough to let him know he will have an actual headstone soon and then scold him for buying the PT cruiser.

I had a light blue Ford Pinto station wagon when Patrick and I met. It had been a new car once, but by the time I could drive, it had been driven by several family members. One year my mom, Dawan, Denny, and I took it to Oklahoma and Arkansas, a minimum of two days of driving in the summer, with no air conditioning!

Patrick didn't own a car when we met. He had to borrow whatever communal car he shared with his brothers if he wanted to drive. He eventually bought a series of used vehicles that got him through college. A few years after we met, I bought my first new car, a 1988 Mazda 323, and I appreciated it! Patrick never got a new car that was his alone. Every new car we had would be mainly driven by me. So I was determined that my kids would learn to appreciate having a good car too.

Some people say they won't buy cars for their kids because they don't want to spoil them. We got them cars because it made our lives easier. Have you ever driven by a high school during drop-off or pickup time? It's chaos!

I can't remember exactly when we got Sierra a car, but I think it was at the start of her junior year. We found a 1997 Saturn, which I thought was perfect since it was only one year younger than her. She was thrilled to have a vehicle. Patrick made her sign a contract, which I found in the China cabinet drawer after he died.

RULES

1. No one may drive the car besides you unless we give permission.
2. This is a third family car, and you will be expected to help your family by:
   a. Taking your sister to school
   b. Picking up your sister from school or practice unless you make prior arrangements
   c. Running errands for your family
4. You will keep the car clean inside and out.
5. You will attend mandatory training sessions with your father on car care and maintenance.
6. No more than four people will be in the car at one time.
7. No cell phone use while driving.
8. Arriving late to school will result in a one-week suspension of car use.

No one under 18 may ride in the car without our permission.

The contract makes me laugh a little because he tried hard to be strict, but he didn't really follow through. I think Sierra did end up following most of the rules, but 2, 3, and 4 are doubtful.

I know for a fact there were no monthly training sessions on car maintenance, although I wish there had been. We did like her having a car, and it was great having her take over driving Camille to school!

Camille did not start driving until halfway through Sierra's first year of college. So we had to again take on the task of driving Camille to school. Camille knew it was a hassle, so she spent her rides home from afternoon sports practice campaigning for us to buy her a car. Patrick thought this was a perfect opportunity to joke with her. So if he turned the corner and there was a car in front of our house, *any* car, he would tell her that we got her a car! Then he would open his glove box and hand her the "keys." The "keys" were a hammer that was inexplicably in his VW bus.

One day, he texted me a picture of a PT Cruiser convertible. The car looked like it was in excellent shape. He told me they were asking $4,700, which was way more than I thought we should spend on a first car. I asked if it was for him, and he said, "No, Camille." He took it for a test drive, and the owner lowered the price. He seemed to really like Patrick. We finally agreed to get the car, and Patrick excitedly told me the story about the "I got you a car" game. I'm pretty sure that Patrick, who rarely, if ever, made impulse purchases, just wanted the car so the story could have a happy ending!

The next day, I picked the car up and took care of the Department of Motor Vehicles paperwork. Then I parked the car in front of the house and waited inside.

Patrick could barely contain himself when Camille started her car campaign discussion! When they turned the corner, he told her he got her a car. She rolled her eyes. He told her to get the "keys" out, and she played along by pulling the hammer out. This time, the hammer had a key ring attached. Camille was confused and cautiously walked up to the car. She unlocked the doors, peered into the windows, then realized I was filming her and casually walked away. She *was* very excited, but did not want that caught on the video.

The car was Camille's, but we all knew she shared it with Patrick. We all enjoyed taking it to the beach or driving around with the top down. I forgot to mention that the car had 183,000 miles on it!

Patrick and I had rented a convertible to celebrate our first anniversary and drove to Morro Bay. We had recently bought our first house, so renting the convertible was extravagant, but worth it. We had a great time driving down the coast.

Patrick didn't talk about wanting a convertible, which wasn't surprising since he rarely mentioned wanting anything. When he saw the PT Cruiser, though, he really wanted to get it, even though we knew it would likely have issues. I'm glad we did buy it! In 2015, we celebrated our 23rd anniversary in Pismo and took the Cruiser with us. I took a picture of him as we drove down the coast with the top down. During that trip, we drove into San Luis Obispo to go to Patrick's favorite sandwich place, the Lincoln Deli. They had great sandwiches and a vast selection of craft beer. We stopped there anytime we visited. He must have been really excited to be there on this day, because we were only there for a few minutes when someone came in and yelled that someone's convertible was in the middle of the street! Patrick had failed to put the car into park and didn't put on the parking brake either! Luckily, no one was harmed, and no damage was done.

Later in the summer, we celebrated Mom and Pop's 50th anniversary in Cayucos. The girls drove the Cruiser to the coast with their cousins, Caitlin and Gianna. Once they hit Highway 1, the top came down again, and they had a great time too!

Sierra, Caitlin, Gianna, and Camille teNyenhuis (the shadow is Patrick)

Last group photo at Mom and Pop's (Nona and Opa's) anniversary celebration

Back Row: Amy, Dan, Danell, Patrick, Gabe, Jen, Dina, Jeff, Tina, and Matt

Front Row: Gabriel, Gianna, Zachary, Sierra, Camille, Nona, Opa, Caitlin, Dominic, Anthony, Desmond, Olivia, Ella, and Andrew

The rest of the time, the car was mainly used to get Camille to and from school. We immediately noticed it ran through oil quickly, so we knew there was some sort of leak. Patrick also mentioned something likely needed replacing, but I have no idea what it was. He showed Camille a little bit about the oil, but nothing major. He taught her to watch the temperature and regularly checked the engine to keep the car running.

After Patrick died, for the first few weeks and months, I knew I should take care of many things, and the Cruiser was on that list. Frankly, I didn't care about any of it. Eventually I would start caring that the pool was turning green and that I needed to handle routine car maintenance, but that was several months down the road. I couldn't remember when the oil had been changed in any of the cars, so I finally just took them all in. After that, I put oil in twice over the next eight months!

A while back, the registration renewal came in the mail, and I had a sinking feeling that it would need a smog check. I also suspected it wouldn't pass. I waited until almost the last minute to take it in, because it was easier to wait until school was out. I had them change the oil first; of course, it was extremely low. I was not surprised when the technician came out to tell me it didn't pass. He seemed to feel bad telling me, so I tried to explain why I wasn't surprised, and that's when I felt the tears threatening.

Our loss of Patrick is so acute at times when I remember just how much he took care of us and what a great job he did. And I do feel more independent, but I also miss him and everything he did.

I must now decide how much I will spend on the Cruiser before it becomes a money pit. It's not the most dependable car, but it has been a great first car for Camille. Mainly, I don't want to sell something Patrick enjoyed so much. For now, I will keep my options open!

Update: I held onto that car for a few more years and then passed it on to my niece, Katie. She drove it for a short time, and then it was passed on to another family member. I'm not sure if they still have it, but I'm glad it got a lot of use and made for a great Patrick story.

ENTRY 59

Most people consider cleaning out their garage a dreaded chore. For me, it is a treasure hunt! Our garage has room for two cars and an extra space for storage. We have always parked our cars in the garage, so it wasn't a complete nightmare. Parts of it were, though!

We used to have a short fence in front of the cars. There is a dog door from the laundry room to the garage and another one from the garage to the yard. The fence was used to keep Aggie from running out when the garage door was open. There was a small gate but the fence was only two and a half feet tall, so we usually just stepped over it. I had fallen over the fence on more than one occasion when my heel caught it, and it wasn't pretty! After Aggie died, I took it down, wanting to organize and throw out unneeded things.

Since the Cruiser was in the shop, today was the perfect opportunity. I didn't finish today, but took an entire carload to Goodwill. My recycling bin is almost full, and the trash can is getting there. I can already see a difference!

Let me tell you, my husband was prepared for just about any kind of home project. He saved everything: cardboard, a broken garage door opener, and a *lot* of empty beer bottles for beer making. A few weeks ago, I filled the back of my car with boxes of beer bottles, and they weighed 68 pounds! That equals five dollars and change, in case you are wondering. I found a few more today and put them in the recycling bin.

I found a whole box of stuff for the VW bus. Matt has been having issues with it, so maybe the box will help. I filled a large bin with beer-making supplies. The girls went through our costumes and condensed them from three boxes to one bin. And, of course, I found a box of treasures.

The box was my stuff this time, so I didn't think I would find much. The first thing I saw was the "Just Married" car sign from our wedding. I also had various magazines, plus newspapers from the first Gulf War, the 1989 Loma Prieto earthquake, and 9/11. I had plaques, trophies and medals, sports award programs, patches never sewn on my letterman jacket, and a T-shirt from Clark Intermediate with the name of every eighth grader from 1981 printed on it. The cap from my college graduation was decorated with the name "Auntie Nellie!" My nephews were my pride and joy back then, and this was what they called me for a while.

The best treasures were two cards and a drawing from Patrick. The first was a handmade card from our first Valentine's Day, which would have been in 1987 (I am including a picture). He was very creative! And the best treasure was another Valentine's card. It says, "For My Wife," but we weren't married yet. The inscription on the inside said: *Danell, I can't wait until this weekend, our wedding, and the rest of our life together. I am living a dream life in a dream world all because of you. I LOVE YOU! Pat*

Handmade Valentine's card

I don't quite know how I got so lucky to find Patrick. I still miss him tremendously and can't believe he's gone. Sometimes I agonize over his last minutes, and I still hope I will wake up from this bad dream. As hard as it is, at the same time, I am profoundly grateful that I had so much time with him. Finding these little hidden treasures reminds me how deeply he loved me and what a great life we had together. That's what I will go to sleep dreaming about—all the beautiful times!

ENTRY 60

I NEED A PATRICK FUNNY – JULY 6, 2017

My friend, Dawn Brown, lost her father today. I never met him and have only really known her since Patrick died. She has been a good friend. One of the first things she told me was that Patrick was one of her work crushes! I immediately bonded with her because he was my work crush too! Patrick was the kind of guy people had crushes on. I was okay with this because I knew I had his heart. In the short time I have known Dawn, I have come to realize that she was extremely close to her father, and I know she must be in a lot of pain now.

Dawn enjoyed Patrick's sense of humor, and we've enjoyed sharing stories of his antics from the other side of his life (home vs. work). I am truly blessed to have met her. Today, she told me she needed a Patrick funny, so I shared this story with her!

Letter from Dan Snider Shortly after Patrick's Death (with Dan's Permission)

Dear Danell,

I heard about the tragic news. I am writing to you with a heavy heart. Laura and I are extremely saddened.

Since I heard on Wednesday afternoon, Laura and I have prayed for comfort for you and your daughters. Memories of Pat have been often in my mind in the last few days.

I would like to share some of my memories, and what Pat meant to me in the decade I was fortunate to have worked with and got to know him.

Danell, I know most people refer to Pat as Patrick, but he told me I could call him Pat as this is how I knew him. I am not doing this at all to show any disrespect but because that is how I knew him, and it seems natural to me.

I last saw Pat at the Clovis Recreation Department approximately two years ago, where he played floorball. I had just finished a practice session with my children's basketball team, and I saw Pat standing by the entrance as I was leaving. We talked for a few minutes, catching up briefly on work and our families. It was nice to talk with him.

Two Saturdays ago (April 9), I took my daughter to shoot basketball at Clovis East around 7:00 p.m. In the parking lot by the soccer and baseball field, my daughter sees this vehicle parked and says, "Dad, look at the van, now that is cool." I believe the vehicle there that night was Pat's as I know his VW van, as I used to see it parked at his outpatient clinic all the time over the last 11 years. I was about to go see if it was Pat but was running late and decided not to. I am disappointed that I did not. On Sunday, April 17, I read the sports page and saw your daughter Camille's name in the paper as part of the Clovis East championship soccer team. Seeing her name reminded me of Pat, you, and your family. Then, last Wednesday, Olga shared with me the news of Pat.

As I believe you know, Pat and I went to the same physical therapy school, and he was a year ahead of me. There was a student in Pat's class who was older at the time named Dennis Fearing. Dennis decided that school was moving too fast while raising a family and ended up finishing in the class I graduated in. I became very good friends with Dennis. I helped Dennis with his studies at times during physical therapy school. He mentioned to me that there was this super smart guy in his class the year before. He told me this guy had a photographic memory, and when a teacher asked a question, this guy would give a speech like it was coming from a textbook. And his name was Patrick teNyenhuis. Dennis was extremely impressed by Pat. As you may also know, I ended up working with Pat at the VA because I also received a scholarship from the VA and owed them time.

I greatly appreciated Pat and your kindness toward me when I began working at the VA. I will never forget coming to your house for several parties and Pat organizing my local bachelor party. I am grateful to you both for being at my wedding in Las Vegas. I also remember going to dinner with you and Pat, I believe, in the Tower District and seeing Mission Impossible.

As I read an article in the paper recently about Pat and his joy of brewing, playing the banjo, and floorball, it made me smile. I remember Pat playing his banjo at lunchtime in this small office next to my desk at work. As I understand it, he became quite an accomplished banjo player. I remember when Pat began to play floorball, and now I read that he was on a traveling team. I also remember how much Pat loved his beer.

Another thing Pat loved that comes to my mind every time I think of him is his VW van. I remember when he purchased it how happy he was, and all the work he told me he put into refurbishing it. That vehicle is a part of who he was. I remember when Pat shared the news of when you were pregnant with both of your children and the smile he had. When you were pregnant with Sierra, Pat told me that "he slipped one past the goalie." Pat's dry sense of humor is something that I missed a lot when he left the VA.

After I graduated from PT school and began working at the VA, I had to take a licensure exam. I took the licensure exam several months after starting my work at the VA. I had to drive to Los Angeles to take it; there was no internet at the time. Pat knew I was nervous about finding out the results, and at that time, the results came 4–6 weeks later in the mail. Pat stated to me on several occasions that the easiest way to know you passed is if you receive a yellow envelope. He stated that people who failed received a white envelope. I am usually not that gullible, but Pat sold it real well. The day I received my exam results and saw a white envelope, I was crushed until I actually opened the envelope and found out that Pat messed with me. Pat had shared priceless stories with me about his first year at the VA before I got there and his interaction with the physical therapist I replaced. They are not appropriate stories to share at this time, but I still bust up laughing when I think of them.

Although Pat had only one year more experience than me, I felt he was a mentor to me. Pat began the casting program at the VA and taught me how to do them. Since then, I have taught many people. The thing I admired about Pat was his work ethic. He was always at work on time and worked his full shift without cutting corners. He never cheated the VA out of one minute of work. He had the highest integrity and was extremely ethical. Pat walked the talk, so to speak. It was easy for me to want to work with someone like that. I have been around many physical therapists over the years, and there is no one better than Pat!

I will greatly miss Pat, and I will never forget him. He was part of my work life for 12 years. I feel honored and privileged to have known him. Laura and I pray for you and your daughters. God bless you and your family.

Sincerely,

Dan Snider

I am so grateful to have stories like this to share and remember Patrick. He was Pat when I met him too, and for the next 14 years. In 1999, or sometime shortly before, he decided that Patrick was a more grown-up name and decided that he would be "Patrick in 2000." At the time, this annoyed me, but once Patrick was committed to something, resisting was pointless. I changed to Patrick like everyone else; now, it is how I remember him.

ENTRY 61

WHAT WOULD PATRICK DO? – JULY 14, 2017

I'm sure I've mentioned how much we enjoy imagining how Patrick would react in different situations. He had such a crazy sense of humor, and we all knew him so well that it's not hard to predict how he would react to particular situations. I used to be embarrassed or horrified at his reactions, but now I miss the constant entertainment. Predicting his reaction is my way of keeping his memory alive. The bonus is that smiling and laughing are easier and less painful than crying.

The summer after Patrick died, my sister Dawan suggested we join her family on Catalina Island for their annual vacation with her husband's family. It was the kind of distraction we needed, and we had a great time.

We went amid the *Pokémon Go* craze and spent a lot of time chasing Pokémon. It helped us work off all of the yummy dinners and snacks. If you're unfamiliar with the game, it involves using your smartphone and walking around to find virtual characters and catch them. I realize many people thought it was a ridiculous way to spend time, especially for a middle-aged mom like me! I didn't care because it made me smile!

At some point, it occurred to me that Patrick never knew about this game, and I mentioned to the girls that he would have had a field day with it.

First, we would have had a long discussion to explain the game to him. It would be a serious discussion, but he would be mocking us the whole time. When he "understood" the game, he would probably then suggest that he play it with us. We would remind him for the thousandth time that he did not have a smartphone. He would reply that he had three and then try to get one of us to give him one of those three phones. And there would be no way we would let him touch our phones because who knew what he might do with them?!

When he realized we wouldn't give in, he would announce that he could play on his flip phone. Then, he would proceed to play an exaggerated version of the game. His version might involve climbing a tree, hopping up and down, or using stealth moves. And I'm sure his version would have special Pokémon that only he could catch. They would have names like Alutnarat, Booger, and Diputs. Or maybe Patrick would call them Nystagmus or Syncope (two names he actually proposed as baby names). We all had a good laugh imagining his reaction, which made playing the game even more fun!

We just returned from our second trip to Catalina with the Utechts and Brandlins. On this trip, we added a few teNyenhuis kids to our entourage. Sierra has a "twin" cousin, Dominic. They were born on the same day in the same hospital, and Monday was their twenty-first birthday. Catalina was the perfect place to celebrate. We had a great time!

This year was easier than last year. I didn't seem to notice every single happy couple, and I didn't cry at all. I'm not going to say that I didn't miss Patrick. I miss him daily, especially when I'm having a great time because he should be there too, right? It's just a little easier to bear now.

I saw a No Turkeys Allowed sign in Catalina. I also remember seeing it last year, but it didn't catch my attention. This year, I was walking by it alone, and people were sitting in the yard it was in. I was almost overcome by a sudden urge to ask them why I couldn't bring my turkey there. Then I thought of Patrick and knew he absolutely would have said something. He would have started a crazy rant about discriminating against turkeys. The people would have thought he was crazy. I would have needed to drag him away in embarrassment. I never thought I would miss that, but I would give anything for him to annoy me now. He was crazy and unforgettable, making it easy for me to imagine him in situations that never happened. He still makes me laugh, and laughter is good.

ENTRY 62

When you have spent 30 years with someone, it's as if they are part of you. It's been almost 15 months, and I still can't get used to Patrick being gone. I was sitting here working on a paper and had a grammar question. My first thought was that I would ask Patrick. My mind just went there, and it seemed my subconscious didn't realize he was gone. Of course, I remembered immediately, but for half a second, I forgot that I was a widow, and I experienced that familiar comfort that was my prior life.

I now follow several grief blogs and belong to a few online grief groups, including the Option B Facebook group and Widowed Village, an online community for Soaring Spirits International. I read other people's stories all the time. I find comfort in communicating with other people who understand. All group members grieve differently, making you realize there is no "one way" to do it. I am still fighting the unconscious feeling that society expects me to be cured of grief at some point. In my everyday life, I don't allow myself to express the full depth of my feelings. Part of the reason is to protect those who love me. I still remember the day Patrick died; I went into my bedroom a few times to change clothes, use the restroom, or just get away for a minute. Each time I went in there, I would look at my bed and think about how easy it would be to curl up there and stay there for the rest of the day. I wanted to do that, but I knew I just couldn't because I wanted to stay strong, and I didn't want to worry anyone.

I still have times that I feel like that. We had a great break in Catalina last week, but it was hard to come home. Before I left, I found out that Patrick's headstone was almost finished, so I anticipated it would be installed soon.

The cemetery received it last week, but they told me it will be another four to six weeks before they install it. I have been warned that seeing it the first time will be hard. I've seen a photo, but heard it is different when it is actually there. I am a little anxious about it, but I also think it will be another closure. If it makes me cry, that will probably be a good thing because I don't think I do enough of that now.

It's tough to write about being sad and missing Patrick. I want to make people smile and laugh. I want to be strong, but I also want to be honest. I miss Patrick every single day, but some days are more challenging. I can truthfully say it has gotten better. I have a decent life and a lot of reasons to be grateful. But at the end of the day, I am faced with the prospect of spending the rest of my life without him. I don't think I will ever get used to that.

ENTRY 63

I was driving today, and it occurred to me that everything I was wearing was purchased after Patrick died. My clothing, watch, and the ring on my right hand. Even my purse, phone, and the car I was driving were purchased "after." It's such an odd feeling. I look slightly different too, but he would still recognize me. Still, it takes a long time for things to change this much. In the last week, I finally took his name off joint credit accounts, which hadn't been a huge priority for me. I didn't realize that he was the primary cardholder on some of them. A day or two later, an online order didn't go through. After finally calling the company, I realized that removing his name caused the account to be closed. I only had a small balance because I use it to get reward points and pay it off each month. I had to listen to an extended disclosure explaining how I wasn't responsible for the charges. I finally interrupted to tell them I wanted to pay it off and reapply in my name. I guess I have been committing fraud all this time. I'm still learning new things about being a widow. I probably should have changed everything long ago, but I did the necessities and dealt with others when ready. I am lucky in this respect, as some widows don't have the luxury of letting things sit like that. For many widows, losing their husbands has a terrible financial impact. Those whose spouses had long illnesses have used up any savings to pay for medical bills and loss of income. Many couldn't afford life insurance. I am grateful that Patrick could, which has at least made things easier. When the accounts were closed, I realized what a bind a widow or widower could be in if they suddenly lost access to credit accounts.

I decided running a free credit report on him would be a good idea. And I *could not* remember his social security number! I couldn't believe it. I've had that number memorized for years! It was just a momentary lapse, but another reminder of how much has changed. Luckily, there were no red flags in the credit report.

I'm sure there will continue to be changes, but hopefully, they can continue to happen gradually. Change can be good, but holding on to some of the familiar is comforting.

ENTRY 64

STEAM DONKEYS - AUGUST 21, 2017

Patrick, Mike, and Abdul

Yesterday, I marked 16 months without Patrick. I've been in a pretty good place emotionally, but at the same time, I still miss him. I love that I can hear his voice anytime I want on videos. I was watching videos on Patrick's YouTube channel, Patrickt9. The videos are perfect memorials because they capture Patrick's sense of humor. "M.T.A." is a standard bluegrass song that he's played for years. I love his corny joke at the beginning and his singing. I sang in the choir for years, which made me a little critical, and early on, I didn't exactly enjoy his voice (I know that's awful to say). After years of practice, he had a nice voice. His bandmate, Abdul, has a great voice too, so he took the lead on many songs, but Patrick is singing this one.

I enjoy watching the "Peace, Love, and Understanding" video, which highlights his improved banjo skills. They usually followed that song with "Little Sister," and I could tell he was happy to play it too.

I love telling the story of how Patrick met Abdul Kassir. My sister and brother-in-law met Abdul at work, and they became great friends with him and his wife, Shannon. Dawan and Abdul both have birthdays in February, and in 2012, they had a combined party. Abdul's son plays in a bluegrass band called The Creak, and they were going to be playing at the party.

Dawan wanted Patrick to meet Abdul, and Patrick was excited that he could bring his banjo for a jam session afterward. The party was nice, with great food and drinks, and the band was great. Later, they all played for a long time. As we drove home, Patrick told me, "I know the party was for Dawan and Abdul, but I feel like it was especially for me; I had so much fun."

After that, Patrick and Abdul regularly got together to jam, eventually calling themselves Grass Half Full. The following February, we were talking, and I mentioned that Dawan and Tom were in Hawaii. He said, "I *know!* They took Abdul with them!" I laughed and said, "Well, it was for his birthday." And he said, "I know, but it is *our* anniversary!" That pretty much summed up how much he enjoyed Abdul's friendship. They continued playing together and even had a gig or two.

Dina and Jeff arranged for them to play at the Central Sierra Historical Society and Museum in Shaver Lake, California. While there, they were asked if they knew any songs about logging or the Shaver Lake area. Since there weren't any songs, Patrick sat down with Jeff and gathered some area history, and then, over a few weeks in early 2013, he wrote eight songs. They renamed themselves Steam Donkeys after both the machine used in logging and one of the songs he had written. Patrick designed a T-shirt logo and had T-shirts made.

One evening, they were practicing, and I came across an email from Mike Kuhl, my cousin Keith Puett's best friend, whom we consider family. Mike wanted to know if Patrick still went to monthly bluegrass jam sessions. I told him that he mostly played with a friend, and I was sitting on the couch just then listening to them. I asked why he was asking. Mike replied that he finally bought a stand-up bass and wanted to play it. I told him he should come over right now. Then I told the guys, and they said," We need a bass player; tell him he's in the band!" He didn't come that night, but they eventually got together, and the band became three.

They had a lot of fun for the next few years, mostly just jamming together, but they played at least five times in Shaver and once in Clovis.

Abdul moved to the Los Angeles area, so they weren't playing as often, but had a concert scheduled for June 2016. Like everyone else, they were devastated when Patrick died.

Abdul recorded a video for the memorial service to be included with the slide show. You can find videos of Abdul on YouTube under the channel @banjofy.

He sent the link the Sunday after Patrick died. That Sunday happened to be the same day as the season premiere of *Game of Thrones*, a show that Patrick, the girls, and I had watched together. We had all been at Dawan and Tom's, but the girls came home early to watch the premier. They were thrilled that the character Jon Snow was brought back to life by Melisandre, the Red Priestess. When I got home, I watched Abdul's video on the couch with them. It was very emotional, since we could see how much Abdul was hurting. After it ended, we all sat there crying. After a few minutes, I was getting worried that they were still crying. Sierra wiped her eyes and said, "I just wish the Red Lady would bring Dad back too." We all looked at each other and started laughing. It was the kind of thing their Dad would say. I knew we were going to be all right.

Here's a message posted by Mike's wife, Dawn, on the day of the funeral, and a picture of the band's T-shirt.

 Dawn Morris Kuhl with **Danell Boyles TeNyenhuis**.

April 27, 2016 at 12:02 PM · 🔍

Said goodbye to a dear friend today. Patrick was funny, smart, witty, sarcastic, unconventional, and truly a sweet man who loved his family with a passion. I think he would have been shocked and surprised at the standing room only service and would have found some smart aleck response to cover up how touched he would have been to know that so many people loved him and were touched by his life.

Ps.. This shirt was designed by Pat for his bluegrass band, Steam Donkeys. In honor of Pat, Google steam donkeys. He would be thrilled that you did!

RIP, my friend.

ENTRY 65

MAYBE IT'S TIME – AUGUST 25, 2017

So, despite repeatedly saying I wouldn't, I set up a dating profile! I might be trying to scare people away with my description of myself, but I have to start somewhere, right?

Writing has become such a part of me that I *have* to write, even if I'm afraid to say things. I hesitated to write about setting up a profile because I didn't want it to sound like an ad. But I must also let people know I might be ready for dating.

I come with a lot of baggage! I haven't dated for 30 years, and back then, I didn't "date" that much. I went on a handful of dates before I met the two boyfriends I ever had. The second one was Patrick! So I don't even really know how to do this.

Some people feel that if you meet your true love, that is it; you will be with them for eternity. That is a romantic thought, and I will always love Patrick. But I do feel you can love more than one person. And I think heaven is different than we could imagine. There is no jealousy. Patrick and I may have had conversations about this, although we didn't discuss much about dying. I can picture him saying something like, "Maybe you will find a guy who is cooler than me!" So, even before I considered dating, I've always known I had Patrick's blessing. He loved me and wanted me to be happy. I will have no guilt about finding someone new.

At the same time, I won't set Patrick aside while I date. He will always be a huge part of my life. If someone is insecure about that, they probably should not date me.

Recently, my mother-in-law, Barbara, told me, "You know, Pop and I don't expect you to be alone forever." Of course, I knew this without being told, but I told her how much it meant to have their blessing. I also told her I would only date someone who realized that the teNyenhuis and Prandini families are part of the package. They will always be my family. So, if you would not be happy spending part of Christmas Day with my late husband's family, you probably shouldn't date me because that's where I will be!

I would love to find someone to share my life with, but I don't *need* to have someone. If I spent the rest of my life as Patrick's widow, the memories of our great love could be enough to sustain me. I would still be sad that he was gone, but I am not going to date just for the sake of having someone by my side.

My profile currently mentions that I am a widow and am unsure if I'm even ready to date. So that will probably scare off most people. And for now, that's fine.

ENTRY 66

I think that this online dating thing is turning into a very brief experiment! It's turning out to be a lot of work with minimal reward. I decided since I know a few other widows and some single people, I could share my experience and some pointers. So far, my experience does not include dates, and I think I'm okay with that!

Photos – I don't have access to the pictures women post, but I'm guessing women put more thought into them. Guys seem to think we will be attracted to their motorcycles, cars, or a picture of the mountains. At least a third of the images are blurry! Who doesn't have access to a camera that can take a clear picture? The strangest phenomenon is the pictures from the nose up, showing half of their head. Is this some secret mating ritual that I don't know about? Oh, and sunglasses! Yes, I would like to see your eyes. And finally, did you mean for your picture to look like you want to kill someone? Because I'm a little bit afraid of you and that's not a quality I'm looking for!

Spelling and grammar – Could you use spell check? Are you trying to fit in so much information that there is no room for punctuation?

Scammers – I'm not 100 percent sure what the scam is, but I think it involves making you fall madly in love and then sending them all your money. Do people really fall for this? Here are the clues I have found so far:

1. Their profile description is very flowery. A flowery profile alone is not a dead giveaway, but I'm not buying it if their messages are also flowery.
2. They live far away. I think the intent here is you can't meet face-to-face until you send them all your money so they can afford to visit.
3. They immediately want to directly communicate outside the app and ask for your phone number. I haven't given anyone my phone number yet and probably wouldn't unless we met for coffee.
4. They want your email address to send you more information and "pictures." Then, if you give them a disposable email, they ask for Gmail. Dude! I know you are sending me some kind of virus; I'm not falling for that! And I don't want pictures you can't post on your profile!
5. English does not appear to be their first language. The way they speak does not make sense. They are using English, but not in a way that you or I would. Example: "I'm not looking for a perfect relationship or a perfect love. Humans aren't flawless, and I expect her to exhibit one." Huh??
6. Their occupation or profession is unusual. Some of the ones I saw: Real State, Worker, Good Worker, Commander of NATO Special Forces on the West Coast (I'm not even kidding)!

I'm sure I am missing some clues, but those are the most obvious.

Dating Sites: I joined five. Don't judge me. Here are my opinions:

Tinder – This one appears to be mainly a hook-up app, so I did not join it.

OKCupid – I joined this first; a friend suggested it. She liked it because you answer a *lot* of questions with the option to answer more. Then, it gives you a compatibility percentage. I found that number questionable, since some of the "high matches" had only answered a few questions. I got messages from many people I was not interested in, so maybe I'm picky. I messaged one person. He messaged me back to let me know he was working and would get back to me, which I thought was nice. He replied a day or two later with a copy of one of my pictures, and the message was "Sexy." I said, "Really? That's your response?" He didn't appreciate my sarcasm. He told me he didn't have time for sarcasm and games.

Bumble – I joined Bumble a day after joining OKCupid. The appeal of Bumble is that the ladies have to initiate conversation. This app does not show me a list of who I "liked," so I probably liked some people more than once. The profiles are minimal, so it seems to be more about looks. I have not messaged anyone on this site, and don't go on it much.

Zoosk – I googled dating sites and found a review section. Zoosk was one of the more highly recommended sites. It has less information than OKCupid but more than Bumble. I think the people here tend to be real because the site uses software to verify your photos, phone number, and social profiles (but you don't share the phone number or social profile on the site). It's a pretty good app. Still, I only got messages from people I was uninterested in and did not send any.

Match – This is one of the more popular ones, and it seems to do at least some verification. It has a lot of features that I like too. I messaged a few people. This might be the site I stay on, but I haven't decided.

Plenty of Fish – This app touts itself as being a conversation starter. When you join, the paid members can see that you are new. I got so many messages the first few days, and some seemed at least a little promising.

Ultimately, I think it was primarily scammers and people I was not attracted to.

So that's my review. I prefer to wait and find someone in the real world. I am having fun identifying the scammers, so I might stay on for the entertainment value. I advise you to be very aware and assume everyone is an imposter!

ENTRY 67

Eighteen months and four days later, I still have outstanding tasks on the death paperwork list. I never realized how intertwined our lives were. I receive electronic statements on every account that offers them, so I don't see the constant reminders in the mail—things like bank accounts needing to be changed because he had one in his name only. I change things like auto insurance, AAA, and Costco because it saves money, at least theoretically. A few things were only in my name because I handled all the bills. However, we always seem to make the husband the primary account holder, and when the primary account holder dies, you sometimes have to close the account.

Today, I called Pacific Gas & Electric, and it took me two minutes to take Patrick's name off the account. I was surprised it was so easy. I usually prefer to make calls when I'm alone. I'm not doing anything secretly, but it's a sad task that I don't want to subject anyone else to.

Sometimes, I'm not alone, like when the girls and I were checking out at PetSmart, and they pulled up our Pet Perks account and verified that it was in Patrick's name (so I had them change it right then).

I previously mentioned trying to close one of our joint credit cards. When I called to close it, there was a $72 balance, and I paid it over the phone. Somehow, it was a credit, so they sent a check to "The Estate of Patrick teNyenhuis." There is no estate because he had no will. So then you have to figure out what to do with the check. Luckily, I asked my fellow widows, and they said just to call and request a new check in my name. I finally did that today, and it was as easy as they said.

I'm sure Patrick would laugh that getting his name off things is so much work. He would find something like that funny and would joke about it being hard to get rid of him. He would probably want me to emulate him when I made the phone calls and harass the people for no particular reason, but I can't bring myself to do that.

So now I'm down to only a handful of accounts. One is the home loan, and they want a copy of the death certificate, which is funny since the title is now in my name. I have plenty of copies of the death certificate since the funeral home advised me to order 10 or 12 of them. But I drag my feet when I need to send snail mail. One of my credit card companies once wanted paperwork to change my name. So, 24 years later, that credit card still says Danell Boyles. Maybe I will change the home loan, or perhaps not. Maybe I like having these outstanding items? I'm in no rush. No matter what, Patrick will always be a part of me.

ENTRY 68

My phone rang today and I didn't recognize the number, but it looked familiar. I answered, and it was the Assistant DA who handled the case. He wanted to update me. The man who hit and killed Patrick has been in a residential program. He has a hearing coming up. He has fully complied with the program, and his drug tests have all been negative. He will likely be released next week and be home in time to spend Christmas with his family. As a future licensed professional clinical counselor, I hope treatment works. As a human being, I am happy that his children might see their father for Christmas. As a mom and a widow, my heart breaks.

Here's the thing: Nothing is going to bring Patrick back. And I have said all along that the only amends this individual could make would be to become a better person. Keeping him locked up will not change anything.

As my whole world has changed, and I have been continuing my education, I'm a different person. I believe there needs to be law and order in society. I think that this person made poor choices in his life that led to my husband's death. But I don't believe he is a murderer. And I think our society has a severe problem with drug and alcohol addiction. Punishment does not cure addiction.

I have so many conflicting emotions right now. I would love more than anything just to wipe this whole part from my memory. My brother told me today that I was stronger than him, and I'm not sure that is true. I just file away all those feelings I don't want to deal with. I function pretty well. And I am truly happy most of the time. But you can't avoid the aftershocks.

I'm allowing myself a few tears tonight. I don't think I will go to the hearing. My presence will not change anything. I've already said what I needed to say. I will focus on my girls, who are both home for Christmas, and on moving forward with my life. I genuinely hope this person has learned something from this and will dedicate his life to doing something positive. But I will follow my brother's advice today: "I wouldn't give him any more free rent in your head. He's either going to change or go back to jail; we can't choose."

ENTRY 69

A BIT MORE CLOSURE – DECEMBER 22, 2017

Today was the final court appearance regarding the collision that caused Patrick's death. The man who hit and killed him has completed the diversion program with negative drug tests. He did everything that was required, so he was released. We don't have to like it. We don't have to agree that it was adequate. I am relieved that it is over. I stayed with my choice not to attend. I am grateful that my brother, Denny, and sister, Dawan, agreed to be there to represent Patrick. I know it was hard for them. I am also thankful that Denny wrote an eloquent letter to the judge (included in the Appendix). We know it didn't make a difference, but we just wanted it on the record.

I will move forward knowing I will not get any more calls updating me on the case. No matter how much progress I make, those calls always have a way of pulling me back, so it does bring me a measure of peace to put the case behind us.

ENTRY 70

Traumatic experiences never really leave you. I tend to downplay my trauma, since it's not a pleasant topic. I survive by filing it away and controlling the time I spend thinking about it—usually, this coping method works.

My class assignment this week was on crisis counseling. Almost every week, I have to write a research paper. I have to find references to support what I write about. Finding references is sometimes easy; other times, it's like pulling teeth. Last week, I found 10 to 15 articles. This week, I had the bare minimum of three.

Sometimes, I will find articles irrelevant to my current assignment, but I save them for future reference. I am interested in grief and trauma counseling, so I have saved many articles on those topics. This week, I found one on a program in Washington, DC, that provides crisis support and bereavement counseling for families who arrive at a morgue to identify someone who died suddenly from homicide, suicide, or accident. The program interested me, so I was eager to read about it.

To clarify, I did not have to identify Patrick or see him until the funeral home had prepared him for viewing. I didn't go through the process discussed in the article, but as I read it, I still found myself back in that viewing room at the funeral home with my legs crumbling beneath me. I realize I did not have to see him.

Whether or not to view someone after death is a profoundly personal decision; for me, it was essential to have that closure.

There were many moments of trauma that I still relive. The moment I saw the breaking news alert with the words "fatal" and "bicycle" jumping out at me. The phone call to tell Sierra. Carlo handing me Patrick's watch and wedding band. Seeing Patrick's body at the funeral home, then taking the girls in to see him (their choice). These memories aren't endless, and they pop up less frequently now. But usually, I'm caught a little off guard.

Yesterday, I was headed to an early morning appointment with my counselor. I got to Shaw and Locan, and BOOM, it was that day again. I wished I could return to the moment I thought I was driving to find my husband walking his bike with a flat tire. One of the last moments before my life changed.

Today, as part of my interview to become a court-appointed special advocate for foster children, I had to describe a traumatic experience and how I had gotten through it. The interviewer knew my background and clarified that I didn't need to discuss *that* experience. The thing is, I'm okay talking about it, and it gets easier every time. I was able to recount all of the love and support I had that day and explain that my gratitude for that is why I am doing so many things in my life now.

ENTRY 71

I had my usual winter sinus or throat bug the first winter after Patrick died. When that happens, I do home remedies of nasal rinses and use the vaporizer at night. And, of course, memories of Patrick are associated with anything routine and ordinary. He always took good care of me, especially when I was sick. He was a healthy guy and was rarely ill, so I'm sure I drove him crazy with my various ailments.

We bought a lot of vaporizers over the years. I always had difficulty carrying them after I filled them with water, so he always did that for me. A few years before Patrick died, I found the perfect vaporizer! The water tank is detachable and a lot easier to clean. I also have an easier time carrying it. The only problem with the tank is the seal that keeps it watertight. I always had trouble opening the tank, and Patrick also did. We gave up a few times and didn't use the vaporizer. He finally resorted to using a wrench! When I got it out for the first time after he died, I was prepared for the inevitable pity party I would have when I couldn't open it. But I closed my eyes and silently asked Patrick to help me. Maybe I could always do it independently, but I used it for four or five nights in a row and didn't have a single problem opening it!

Although I do it less often now, back then I still talked to Patrick frequently and asked for his help when I needed physical or emotional strength. He never talked back, but I always felt he was sending me strength. I have learned that many people who have suffered a loss like mine are more open to after-death communication.

I have a few songs that I feel Patrick sent to me when I needed to hear them. The one that has the most significance is "Yellow" by Coldplay. This song was playing in my head over and over at one point, and I hadn't intentionally listened to it before that. The words don't all fit, but just the color has meaning. Patrick wore a lot of yellow over the years, and it is the signature color of our nephew, Desmond, who is also our godson. Yellow now makes me think of Patrick.

One day, during the first summer after Patrick died, I was at Clovis Community Hospital for some lab work. On my way back to my car, I passed an older couple, and I was suddenly angry and jealous that I didn't get to grow old with Patrick. Just then, I looked down and saw hundreds of yellow flowers! I had walked into the hospital on the same path and hadn't noticed them. The skeptical part of me pointed out that there was no way Patrick could have suddenly made them appear there. Only God could do that. Finally, it occurred to me that he could have caused me to look down at that moment because he knew the flowers would make me think of him and remind me of how much he loved me.

I also associate hummingbirds with Patrick. My sister, Dawan, told her friend about our loss a few months after Patrick died. That friend, Laurie Smith, happens to have the ability to be a mental medium. She doesn't do it professionally or charge people. She had also lost her husband 18 days after Patrick died, and his name was Pat. If that's not a sign, I don't know what is.

I had never believed in psychics or mediums. I once had my palms read, and I thought it was a little phony. As a Christian, I struggled to reconcile my religion with this type of spirituality. But, like many widows and others mourning a loved one, I was willing to grasp anything to connect with Patrick.

Dawan told me that, as soon as she mentioned Patrick, Laurie told her she could feel him. Dawan asked me if I wanted to speak to Laurie, and I was open to anything. I had a healthy amount of skepticism, but I didn't think it would hurt anything.

Laurie and I initially spoke on the phone and then continued our conversation through text and Facebook Messenger, which makes it easy to refer back to her messages. I felt an immediate connection with Laurie. She told me Patrick wanted me to watch out for hummingbirds. He felt that if I studied their actions, it would give me a safe passage in moving forward. Here is the description of those movements that she gave me:

Calculated angles
Dodging
Quickness in intuition of movement
Zigzag to move out of harm's way
Speed
Thoughtful, active preparation for flight while resting

Laurie commented on the instructions' complexity and asked if Patrick was a mathematician. I explained that he was brilliant and complex and a physical therapist. She said that made sense, and he concentrated on movement and putting each action together to make it work. And she agreed that complex was what she got from him.

Laurie described Patrick's message as "almost like creating a ballet or action plan for you—a higher level than he would give a patient—his plan for you is laced in love and meticulousness. Sounds crazy, but I feel he has worked out this idea to get you moving."

I was smiling at this point because it sounded like a message from my husband. Then Laurie added, "MECHANICS OF THE HUMMINGBIRD!! He likes that term! Intelligent and interesting man!" Her words made me smile broadly. I could hear Patrick saying these things.

She asked if I had a hummingbird feeder, and as I was getting ready to reply, she typed, "He says no, you don't have one." And then, "Buy one online." That sounded just like him. She said that he wanted to "Be my wings." Then she said, "He said to get the non-red hummingbird food because you have to calculate how to mix. It's simple, but he likes the more meticulousness behind it."

Maybe he was messing with me, or she was making this up. He had never talked about feeding hummingbirds. Then, a few weeks later, I got up the nerve to tell my mother-in-law about the medium. She is a devout Catholic, and I assumed she might disapprove. I was surprised when she said that she believed it was possible. I was even more surprised when she told me they always had hummingbirds while Patrick was growing up. My father-in-law used homemade sugar water to feed them, so he would carefully measure the ingredients.

I bought a hummingbird feeder, and I saw a lot of hummingbirds when it got warmer. Sometimes, I would not see them for days, but there would be one when I seemed to need a sign. In September, I was still working when I made a late afternoon appointment to talk to a counselor at the psychology school (Alliant). I was considering returning to school and had been having a hard time with work. I was having a stressful day at work that day, and was in tears when I left for my appointment. I pulled myself together, but I got emotional when I explained my reasons for wanting to return to school.

I was very emotional when I left the counseling appointment. I was also frustrated because I didn't immediately know if returning to school was what I wanted to do with my life. My life had been violently altered, and I desperately hoped to find a new direction. As I got home and pulled into the driveway, I looked up, and a hummingbird was at the feeder. The hummingbird seemed to pause and look at me, and then darted off. I believe that was a sign that I was on the right path.

A month or so later, we went to the first court hearing. When I came home, I sat on the couch by the window and saw hummingbirds at least 10 times that day! That was a hard day, and I appreciated the multiple visible reminders!

I will continue to look for signs. I feel my connection with Patrick is eternal and I know I will continue to see proof.

ENTRY 72

MORE ADVENTURES IN ONLINE DATING –
MARCH 23, 2018

If you are hoping for details about actual online dates, sorry to disappoint you. My online dating experience has been mainly online; genuine encounters with real people have been rare. Lately, I have been on dating sites mostly to have a good laugh! As a community service, I have decided to review a few more sites and give you some tips on identifying fake profiles. Along the way, I will present my top 10 dating profiles. I'm including original grammar, spelling, and punctuation.

#10 – I am a classy and fun Man who takes pride in his family and self. He is the light of my life.

According to the Pew Research Center, one in 10 Americans has used some form of online dating. Of those who participate in online dating, approximately 25 percent find a spouse or partner. I was surprised to learn that the National Academy of Sciences determined that "marriages that began online, when compared with those that began with traditional offline venues, were slightly less likely to result in a marital breakup (separation or divorce)."

#9 – I'm a single father with my two little twins who lives with her nanny

Since so many people use online dating services, I expected that meeting people would be easy. For some reason, this was a little easier at first. Part of the reason it is more challenging now is because I seem to find the same group of men on the same multiple dating sites. I've either screened them out, or they've screened me out. I am having so much trouble because finding real men among all the fake profiles is tough! I suspect that many scammers are focusing on my demographic: the middle-aged widow.

Keeping this in mind, I am very cautious and suspicious.

#8 – I'm calm and down to earth and a well calculated am here to meet new people around the world.text if you look just good. I'm a licensed trader and into freelancing.....there are lots you sure need to know about me

Since my last online dating review, I've tried a few new apps. For security purposes, I pay for a service called BeenVerified. I need a real name or phone number for it to work, and it doesn't always work, but it has been reasonably reliable. If I can pull someone up, I know they are real. These guys might be slightly creeped out by this, but I need to play it safe. I also pay for LifeLock, and I think it works pretty well because I can't pull myself up on the app!

#7 – I'm cool gentle and humble man I hate lies and cheating I'm old enough to play games, I'm for real relationship. My job I'm a business man. My Company is primarily involved in the developing and process-ing of Rare Earth materials in the High purity sector.

Another app I have downloaded is Kik. It's a messaging service, and I think many scammers use it. It is used for human trafficking too, so make sure your teenagers are not using it. I use it if I am suspicious, as it is an easier way to message, and I don't have to give out my phone number. You can also download burner apps that will give you a fake phone number for texting.

#6 – I'm a man who loves her family.

I finally caved and downloaded Tinder. I did this because you log in through Facebook, which will show you if you have mutual friends. The connection with Facebook has helped me identify a few real people, but most of the profiles I find on Tinder do not have any mutual friends. I have stayed on Tinder mainly to collect hilarious profiles! I know many people meet on Tinder, so I think it must just be that the scammers are targeting my demographic.

#5 – Profile name: Phil_Magroin

I also tried EliteSingles. It has been a total dud. Most of the profiles don't have pictures, and there are few local people. There may be fewer scammers, but I usually don't interact with profiles without photos unless they are interesting or funny.

#4 – Am a man of integrity and I respect my pride.

Let's talk about pictures. I hate to focus on appearances. The guys I have met all looked even better in person. And many of the guys don't smile in pictures. If I were around someone a lot and got to know their personality, I might be attracted to them for that. Intellect and a sense of humor are also qualities that I look for. And I have talked to a few guys with no pictures. I was just not attracted when they finally shared their photo, which is awkward. So a picture is preferred.

#3 – Am just a man that wants a woman that has a good sense of human and am a man that can make a woman enjoy everything she desire...But am a man with respect and I like talking dirty am also that type that like to be told the truth and I hate cheating, confusion and fake life

As you can tell from my top ten list, these fake profiles are relatively easy to spot. But there are so many of them; there must be people falling victim to them. I decided to investigate, and many of the scams originate in Nigeria. There are also other places, but Nigeria has the worst reputation for scams.

They establish a relationship with the victim, and then there is usually some kind of crisis where they need money. Or maybe they are trying to meet, and need money for a plane ticket. A few times, I have communicated for a bit with them, but I usually give myself away. The closest I have come to being scammed was one guy who asked if I could buy him an iTunes card. I said no, of course!

#2 – *From a 22-year-old: Will you marry me? I can provide you with free medical and dental; lol*

Aside from the poor grammar, I also identify the scammers by their profession. Most of the time, they say they are in the military. They probably have no idea there are very few active-duty military around here, and certainly not generals. Some say they work for the United Nations.

Then there are engineers, contractors, and doctors. They also seem to select cities randomly. I see many who will put the name of a town that might be on the map but has a tiny population. Or the city doesn't match the occupation. I don't think many United Nations employees live in small California farm towns!

#1 – *I've a great sense of humor, no games and I don't hit my woman*

I don't know why, but that profile just really made me laugh! I didn't include Jesus here, but yes, Jesus loves me, and this I know because he swiped right on Tinder. And he had a very recognizable picture! I hope that this has entertained and informed you. I have one last list: my top five online interactions. For the last three, I copied the conversations to give you the complete picture. Enjoy!

#5 – *Standard greeting from more than one person – "I will like to know you better"*

#4 – *your lips is adorable because the smiling on you bring out the real beauty in you*

#3 – Counselors are equivalent to surgeons????

> Scammer: *So what do you do dan?*

> Me: *I am a student. Working on my master's degree in Professional Clinical Counseling*

Scammer: *Oh that's great! My daughter once told me she love to be a surgeon, I guess that's the same line of profession. Do you have a boyfriend?*

Me: *No. A surgeon requires way more training. You are a pilot? What airports do you fly into?*

Scammer: *I'm a freelancer. I have captained at various airport for over 33 years. I fly private jets for clients on appointment.*

#2 – I've decided to start playing along, I usually can't stay serious for long though!

Me: *So, do you live in the Fresno area?*

Scammer: *Nope. And you*

Me: *I live in Clovis. Where do you live?*

Scammer: *I live in Sanger Cal. Have you ever been there before?*

Me: *Yes, of course. What do you do for a living?*

Scammer: *Cool. Special detective with the United Nations. And you what you doing for a living?*

Me: *Do people really fall for that? If you had ever lived in Sanger, CA you would know that no one with that kind of job would live there.*

Scammer: *Oh yeah, you are right, I like your good sense of humor, most people won't think positively. But presently I'm in Minnesota. Hope it won't bother you?*

Me: *Are you sticking to the special detective story? Did you want me to send you money now or are you going to try to get me to fall in love with you first?*

Scammer: *Sighs. Do you think money is everything, do I ask money from you, you are so rude for that, I will never force you to do what you don't want to do, I'm an elderly person and I know what I want and need in my life. Money can't buy true love, we are both mature here, I know you have talked to millions of guys on here. But you don't have to judge me from your past.*

#1 – Me: *Hello - I'm Danell. How are you?*

Scammer: *I'm Lawrence by name and you*

Me: *I'm Danell*

Scammer: *Nice to meet you. How long have you being on here?*

Me: *I've been being on here for a few weeks.*

Scammer: *What are you looking for on here?*

Me: *I'm looking for a man to take care of me.*

Scammer: *Oh same here but I want a responsible woman. Who will love me for who I'm*

Me: *Do you make good money? I like to travel and get expensive gifts.*

Scammer: *Yes I make good damn money. What about you?*

Me: *I'm unemployed*

Scammer: *I'm a veteran doctor. Ok so how do you earn your living?*

Me: *I find men to take care of me.*

This one blocked me shortly after the last message you see. I didn't get a chance to copy the last interaction. He asked how the kids were, and I said I kicked them out because they were eating too much. And he finally figured out that I wasn't serious.

This whole experience may be a waste of time but at least it has been entertaining!

ENTRY 73

UPS AND DOWNS OF LIFE – JUNE 15, 2018

Camille has wrapped up her first year at UC Davis. She did well, loved the experience, and made new friends. This time last year, I was terrified of letting go, and I know she was also a little apprehensive. I'm so happy she loved her first year there. Patrick would have been pleased about that too. Of course, I really miss him at times like this.

He would have been excited to hear about her year and even more excited to have her home! And he would have loved UC Davis. He would have wanted to ride his bike around campus with her. And he would have made the moving so much easier!

While driving to get her, I had some random flashbacks of the day he died. For some reason, I was thinking about different family members and what it must have been like for them. Matt, Patrick's younger brother, was always the baby of the family. On that day, I gave him one of the most challenging tasks. Early on, when we knew, but not really, I asked him to go pick up his parents. I didn't want them to get a phone call, so I asked him just to go. Matt was very close to Patrick, which made telling his parents even harder. I knew it was a lot to ask, but I also knew he could do it.

I don't know why thoughts like that randomly pop into my head. They make me incredibly sad, and I can't always show it because it's hard to explain. Luckily, it doesn't happen often, and it's not unbearable. It is just part of my life. So I'm kind of used to it, and I don't stay sad for long.

Sometimes, other random things happen. Several days ago, I had a missed call from a blocked number. I didn't even think about who it might be. A year ago, or two years ago, I would have known it was possibly the police or the DA. But not now. Then, yesterday, I answered a call while we were in the middle of moving Camille.

The detective called to ask what I wanted to do with Patrick's bike. I didn't even know they still had it. I think I wondered at first, just like I wondered about his phone and maybe the police report or the autopsy. But I never asked. If I asked, then I would have to make a decision, so I just never asked. And then suddenly, I was asked about the bike he had owned for possibly 20 or more years. The bike that was a huge part of his life. The bike he died on. The call kind of took my breath away. I have learned that I don't have to make immediate decisions. I asked a few questions and told him I would need a few days. My gut said I should let them destroy it. But I knew I couldn't make a snap decision. It was just so weird and unexpected. Before I hung up, I did finally ask about Patrick's ancient flip phone, and he told me that he was returning that also. I still have the charger, but I know it may not even turn on. I'm unsure what will even be on it if it turns on, but I want to see it. And it kind of has sentimental value.

Deciding what to do with the bike was new territory for me. I turned to the only place I might possibly find someone with experience making this kind of decision. I asked for feedback from the Option B Facebook group I had previously joined. The members of the group have all experienced grief and it is a good place to ask questions. The group members gave me some excellent suggestions on whether or not to have the bike returned. Some suggested it might be closure. Others told me I shouldn't let an object hold any power over me. Finally, my brother asked if he could pick it up. He will do something with it to raise awareness, which is a great idea. I let the detective know Denny would pick up the bike and phone.

Despite the unsettling call from the detective, I am happy to have both daughters home for a few months. We have some fun trips planned, and I know it will fly by. Then I will live alone for the first time in 27 years. I enjoyed it the first time, but I usually saw Patrick on the weekends. I think I will enjoy aspects of it now and I also think I will have a lot of things to keep me busy. For now, I will enjoy my summer with the girls!

ENTRY 74

I held my breath as my brother, Denny, opened the back of his SUV. He had told me it wasn't as bad as he expected, but still. Suddenly, there was the bike Patrick had owned for most of our marriage. The bike that he rode through all kinds of weather—to work, for exercise, towing a bike trailer to pick up the girls from daycare. So many years. So many miles.

My husband was a fanatic about working out. I never noticed a bit of fat on him, not even a beer belly, though he definitely would have earned that. He was a faithful Catholic, but working out was his second religion. I know I'm repeating myself, but I can't tell you how ironic it is that he died while working out. It's ironic and unfair. And so preventable.

The front half of the bike looks the same to me. It's well-worn but definitely Patrick's. I notice the seat is cracked and peeling, and I laugh. No self-respecting cyclist would put their rear on that saddle! But Patrick was the anti-cyclist. He didn't need all that fancy stuff—just two wheels, pedals, and maybe some gears. In cycling, his ride would be referred to as a "beater bike." He occasionally confiscated some of my gear, like the expensive headlight with the external battery that didn't survive, or wasn't found after, the collision.

The rear wheel looks like an accordion. It is what you would expect a wheel to look like when a car runs into it. I stare at it for a minute and then turn to bury my head in Denny's shoulder.

There are also three envelopes, all marked with evidence tape. I open the envelope with the phone first. I take it out, and it doesn't look familiar. I'm surprised that it's unfamiliar, and then I see that it says Verizon and realize it's *not his phone!* In the same instance, I know it must be the driver's, and I quickly stuff it back in the envelope. Hopefully, the police still have Patrick's phone. The second envelope is a water bottle. I wondered which bottle he had taken, but I never took inventory. I suspected it would be one of mine, and it was a bottle I got when I participated in America's Most Beautiful Bike Ride at Lake Tahoe. The last envelope was a part of his reflector that didn't look familiar, just a random item you might see on the side of the road.

Denny takes pictures of the bike and sends them to me later. In one, there is an illusion of a normal bike since the tire has retained its shape outside of the twisted wheel. I comment on this to Denny, and he says, "Rubber holds its shape, like a memory of what it should still look like."

This bike is the result of distracted driving. It doesn't matter what the distraction is. The result is the same when you are distracted enough to run into a person, whether they are on a bike, walking down the street, or in another car. The driver did not have alcohol in his system. He had meth in his system, but no one seems to know how much meth is too much. How much meth does it take to make you impaired? According to California, there is no clear definition of drug impairment. I don't think you should drive when any substance impairs you. Maybe someday, the law will agree.

I firmly believe that meth and other activities interfered with this driver's sleep, and ultimately, he fell asleep at the wheel, which is also distracted driving.

So do me a favor in memory of Patrick and the countless individuals who lose their lives yearly: if you are too drunk, high, or sleepy to drive, get an Uber or Lyft. Call a friend. Walk home. Do *not* get behind the wheel. And when you do drive, put your phone down and pay attention to the road. Don't make someone else experience this horror.

We have donated Patrick's bike to the Fresno Cycling Club. The bike has been painted white to be used as a "Ghost Bike" at the annual Ride of Silence to raise awareness of cyclists killed while riding and to support cyclists' right to safe travel.

Patrick's bike at the Ride of Silence

ENTRY 75

When you lose someone unexpectedly, especially with an element of tragedy, you become the center of attention for a while. This strange feeling is not the kind of attention most people hope to get. In the first weeks after Patrick died, it was really pronounced. People felt so helpless, and they would jump at the chance to do something. Having extra help was good, since there were times when I wouldn't have eaten if someone hadn't put food in front of me. The girls noticed it too. Sierra commented about it and said she felt she could ask for just about anything. She even joked a little and said she thought she could ask for something random, like a lint roller, and someone would get it. I shared this story, and the next time her Zia Jen came over, she brought her three or four lint rollers.

All joking aside, it's not the kind of attention we were looking for, and it was good when things got back to normal. And now, we focus a lot more on the good memories. But it's a sad story; inevitably, it will come up many times when you meet new people. It's always a little uncomfortable. You want to tell new friends, but you know it will make them sad. I don't want to minimize the impact, but I want people to know we are doing well. So I always try to find a quick way to explain that this horrible, life-changing event happened, but it is no longer the center of our existence. I'm not sure if that even makes sense. I just think it's one of those things that will always be awkward.

Last Saturday, my sister Denise and I heard her friend's band play. She ran into many friends while we were there, and one came to sit at our table. I'm unsure how it even came up, but Denise told him I was her sister who had lost her husband. It was just a footnote in the conversation, but it changed the entire direction. The friend jokingly scolded Denise for bringing up such a sad topic. I always find it funny when people worry about reminding someone that a loved one died, because there will never be a time when a remark makes me remember I'm a widow; I always know. Denise set him straight and told him we talk about Patrick always, and she knows I am comfortable with it. And again, I think the guy was just teasing her, but I think it's odd that death is such a taboo subject. People just aren't sure how to handle it. I also don't want it to appear that I am bringing it up for them to feel sorry for me. I know that's inevitable, but I sometimes want to apologize for making people feel bad. I know that's silly, but unfortunately, it's just our culture. We all see the elephant in the room, but maybe people will forget he's there if we don't mention it. Really? It's an elephant! I know I don't speak for everyone who has lost someone, but I think, in general, it is better for everyone if we acknowledge that death is a part of life, and so is grief. I will never forget Patrick, and I will occasionally be sad about that. That's just the way it is.

ENTRY 76

WHY WOULD I NEED A SMARTPHONE? – AUGUST 23, 2018

I always wanted Patrick to have a smartphone so it would be easier to send pictures and texts back and forth. And, of course, I wanted to send him cute emoticons! He was anti-mainstream and would never choose to do something just because that's what everyone did. He was also fiercely anti-social media. He didn't want any internet presence, but finally began allowing YouTube videos. He didn't understand the appeal of Facebook. I found some of his fraternity brothers and became friends with them so we would have a way to contact them if he ever wanted to. (I was grateful I made contact with them, since many of them came to his funeral after seeing my posts.)

Once, I noticed that one of them was online and told Patrick he could chat with him. He got on my computer, and they messaged for a few minutes. Then he wanted to know the protocol for ending the conversation. He felt it was kind of impersonal and awkward.

If you knew Patrick, you know he never wanted to be trendy. Sometimes, it seemed like he was against something just to have something to debate about. He always claimed to hate his cell phone and constantly threatened to get rid of it, and I told him I would just buy another one. He liked to keep them as long as possible. I always wanted him to upgrade so he could do things like take pictures and also just to make it easier to text.

I can't remember exactly when he got his first cell phone, but I'm pretty sure I bought it when he was taking the VW bus on a road trip. Breaking down was always a possibility, and I wanted him to be able to call for help. I'm kind of amazed that I ever got him to carry it! He didn't like to talk on the phone that much unless it was to annoy a telemarketer or catch up with a relative or old friend.

Once, he went fishing at Shaver Lake and put his phone in his pocket. He stood up on the boat for something, and the phone dropped into the lake, never to be seen again. He texted or called me from Dina's phone to let me know what had happened. I loaded the girls up and headed to the phone store for a replacement. I knew he would refuse to get one if I waited for him to do it! Unfortunately, smartphones didn't exist back then, or that's what I would have bought him.

His final phone was a flip phone. It was out of style when he got it, and before he died, the cell phone provider sent him messages that they would no longer support his phone.

We liked to tease him about it, and he would act offended. Then he would start on all the reasons his phone was better than ours. I'm sure he had a lot of reasons, and I remember being cheaper was one of them.

He liked to tell everyone how awesome his phone was. He extolled the virtues of the flip phone and bragged about how it folded up so small. The phone *did* have internet access, but the screen was so small I'm not sure how easy it would have been to use.

According to Patrick, the phone's most useful feature was something that he liked to demonstrate, usually while sitting in a restaurant. He would proudly state, "How many of you can put your entire phone in your mouth?" And then he would proceed to demonstrate.

Of course, if he ever wanted to know any trivia or obscure information, he would say, "What are you waiting for? Someone look that up!" And I would tell him he should get his own smartphone. His response? "Why would I need a smartphone? I already pay for three of them!"

Ironically, I think he would have enjoyed the features of a smartphone. He would have liked taking pictures and probably would have enjoyed having better-quality photos of the girls on his phone to show people. And he definitely would have appreciated the easier texting. I used to laugh as he struggled through typing a long text. One time, we were talking about sending a message to Sierra. So he started the painstaking process of hitting each key multiple times. I couldn't help it and gave him a relatively long head start, then I picked up my iPhone, spoke the message into it, and hit send before he could finish. He wasn't amused, LOL.

Camille was the first to point out that Patrick made it through his entire life without getting a smartphone. He would be proud of that.

I've been wondering about that flip phone for two years. I knew it was evidence in the court case, but I never wanted to ask about it. After I initially got the wrong phone, I finally got Patrick's phone back in July. I braced myself not to be disappointed if it didn't work, but I charged it for a few hours, and it worked!

It was a challenge after using an iPhone for so many years. I was surprised that it had Bluetooth and internet access when he used it. I turned off the service after he died, so I can't access that now. Several pictures of the girls also probably didn't exist elsewhere. At some point, I will take the SIM card in to see if there is a way to get the pictures off it.

I don't know why, but having details of those last few days has always been very helpful. Many people had shared their final texts with him, so I didn't think there would be any surprises. Still, I was hoping there might be something.

I wanted to know his last texts and calls sent and received. The final text exchange was between him and me on Monday, April 18. They were ordinary texts about him dropping the VW bus off and me picking him up. The last call he received was later that day when Burnett's Auto Repair called to tell him what was wrong with the bus. The next day, he called me a little after 5:00 p.m. I don't remember exactly what that call was about. And, of course, there was a missed call from me on the morning of the 20th when I was looking for him.

There were no voicemails because he went through a lot of trouble to turn off that feature. In typical stubborn Patrick fashion, he decided that he didn't want to get voicemails. I'm sure he had a very long explanation for why, and I know I knew it at one time, but the memory has faded. If you knew him, you can imagine it was equal parts logical and ridiculous! All I know is that his boss and employees were probably very annoyed about being unable to leave a message!

I looked through the pictures, and they were a pretty good summary of what was important to him. There were a few pictures of me and many pictures of the girls.

I also found quite a few texts in his "drafts" folder. Here is one that he was possibly planning to send out; it's precisely the kind of gem I was looking for!

"Hey, it's Patrick. If you don't know who I am, please disregard this message, as it's going out to my entire address book. After much soul searching, I have decided to abandon my cell phone as it has not substantially improved the quality of my life. Just another inconvenience. Anyway, if you need to contact me, call my wife, she loves her phone more than she could ever love any man and knows how to find me. Peace out."

Patrick *did* create a Facebook account several months before he died. He decided it would be an excellent way to store photos and videos, but he wanted it to be secret. He was annoyed that he needed his own email address, since I was using the one I shared with him. After he created a Gmail account, he started working on his secret Facebook profile. Then he got annoyed with some of the things he was being asked and said it was too complicated. He deleted the account, but was mad that it would take 14 days. Then he tried to delete his Gmail, but they required a forwarding address, so he was angry about that too, and went on a rant about how ridiculous it was. Since his death, many people have pointed out the irony of his significant internet presence now.

ENTRY 77

Bruce and I met on OKCupid in August 2018. I don't remember who contacted the other first, but we both swiped right and started talking on Monday, August 13.

I remember that we switched to phone calls early on, which I enjoyed. Bruce's profile said he lived in Clovis, so I asked him what part of town, and he told me his cross streets were Ashlan and Locan, which also happened to be my cross streets! I think I might have looked out the window at that point. Fortunately, he wasn't a stalker and had lived just across Locan from me for the last four years. In fact, we had lived less than a mile from each other since 2003. Our kids were in different grades, but went to all the same schools together! We made plans to go to dinner that Saturday night, but as we talked more, I suggested we meet for coffee on Friday. I met him at Starbucks, and we were so comfortable that he suggested we go to dinner.

He gave me the option of taking separate cars, but of course, I wanted to ride in his cute little convertible!

Bruce's dating profile picture (we like each other!)

The next night, he picked me up for the dinner date we had planned initially. Once again, we enjoyed each other's company so much that we decided to extend the date and see a movie *(Crazy Rich Asians)*. From then on, we talked multiple times daily and saw each other almost daily, sometimes walking the short distance between our houses. Usually, we would meet in the middle.

I am the first to admit that dating me was a lot! Bruce is an only child and grandchild, so it was somewhat of a culture shock when he met my family. He met the teNyenhuis side first! I tried to introduce him to small groups at a time, but that is a challenge when we spend so much time together. After a month of dating, he met all of my siblings and helped our family move furniture into our family beach house. I introduced him, and he was immediately put to work carrying furniture upstairs and putting things together. We still had shopping to do, so I left him with the guys while Dawan and I went shopping for a few hours. He likes to say I left him for 10 hours, but don't believe him!

Everyone seemed to like him, and that made me very happy! But I knew things were going well when I overheard Tom talking to my dad the following day. The conversation was something like this: "We were trying to do . . . then Bruce said . . . we did this . . . Bruce thought we could . . . Bruce suggested . . . ." You get the picture; he fit so seamlessly into the family!

After returning home, we went to dinner with Sierra and Camille to meet Bruce's youngest daughter, Bethany. We had fun at dinner, then took them to see "our movie," *Crazy Rich Asians.*

Bruce continued meeting more family. Then I took him to the Boyles family reunion, then Ravioli Day, which is an annual tradition of the Prandini family where we gather and make the raviolis we will eat on Christmas Day. He was proud when he could remember a few names, and I would introduce him to more. We spent Christmas Eve and morning with my family, and then I took him to Prandini Christmas. After each big event, I gave him space to decompress. And then he was always ready to meet more people.

After a few months of dating I got to experience a Facebook first. I changed my status to "In a Relationship with Bruce Black." I felt comfortable making this change and confident about our relationship.

Bruce and me, 2019

ENTRY 78

Patrick would have been 52 today. I can't believe this is the third birthday we've spent without him. So much has changed, but it still seems like yesterday. I couldn't be with both girls this year. Sierra has something going on at school. So Bruce and I drove to Davis to be with Camille for Picnic Day, which was a lot of fun!

Camille took us around downtown for a while last night. She was narrating while walking; I'm sure her dad would have loved it. At one point, we realized we were at the edge of downtown and needed to turn back. Then she looked in the window of the building we were walking by, and there was Zoltar! There are always little reminders of Patrick. The Zoltar arcade fortune teller was in the movie *Big* and was the reason Tom Hanks' character turned into an adult. Patrick thought it was a cool-sounding name, so he liked to use it when he called in an order for sandwiches, especially if someone else was picking it up. He always had to be different. When he signed up for the Port of Subs discount card, he put his name as Mr. Sandwich. He once wanted Camille to pick up Port of Subs, and she didn't want to go alone. He agreed to go with her if she would walk in and say, "I am Zoltar." She agreed, and off they went. When they walked in, they said, "For Zoltar?" Camille knew she could probably be off the hook, but her dad wouldn't have let her off that easy, so she said, "I am Zoltar." Patrick went to pay, and when he gave his phone number, the cashier looked surprised and said, "Mr. Sandwich?" Patrick replied without missing a beat, "Yes, and this is my daughter, Zoltar."

That guy . . .

We've had a lovely day so far. Camille loves it here, and I can only imagine how proud he would be of her. I'm glad we have so many great memories of Patrick! Happy Birthday, Mr. Sandwich! I will always love you!!

ENTRY 79

In September, right after I met Bruce, I had a small flood at my house, causing it to be in disrepair for months. I couldn't decide what to do. Should I have it repaired? Should I have additional work done? I thought about remodeling the kitchen, and Bruce suggested I get ideas from model homes. He told me he enjoyed visiting the models, and there were a few he liked. We had a blast looking at the models, and I imagined what the future might hold. Then he asked if I might want to buy a house together someday. I'm sure I had a big grin when I told him I would love that! Then he added that, of course, he would want to marry me. My grin got even bigger!

We started looking at more houses, and I decided not to remodel my kitchen. Instead, I started getting it ready to sell.

Even before the conversation at the model home, we had talked hypothetically about moving in together. Bruce's house was nice, but had limited parking, which would not work for family get-togethers! My house made more sense, but I worried it would be hard for Bruce to feel like it was his home. We decided it would be better to move to a house that was ours together. I worried about leaving the home the girls had spent most of their child-hood in, but I knew they would be moving forward with their lives, and having a little more space would be nice. Bruce's oldest daughter, Brittney, was living out of town with her partner, so we knew she wouldn't be living with us. But we wanted a space for Bethany, his youngest, so we needed at least one more bedroom.

I had known Bruce for 11 months when we moved in together, yet it seemed much longer. There are so many reasons we fell in love. I want to backtrack and tell you what I love about Bruce and our story.

Bruce treats me like a queen. He always opens the car door for me, even if I'm the one driving! And he tells me I'm beautiful every day.

When we started dating, he pulled out a picture of him and his girls at one of the Freedom Elementary father-daughter dances. I pulled up a picture of Patrick and my girls at the same dance! My brother Denny was also there with his girls! Such a small world!

Preparing my house for paint and flooring and putting both houses on the market took time. Bruce's house sold first, and he was waiting for that to happen to make a particular purchase. He was out of town when it closed. When he returned, we went to look at rings, and we were both impatient, so he bought it on June 30. I still consider our first model home visit the actual proposal! When we got in the car, I asked him to put the ring on my finger. Then we FaceTimed my dad so Bruce could officially ask his permission. The camera was on Bruce, and when my dad said, "Of course," I turned it to me and said, "Good answer!" as I waved my ring at him.

Two weeks later, we got the keys to our new home and moved in that Saturday. Although it was summer time, neither of the girls were home for the move. Camille was taking a summer abroad in Spain and Sierra was doing an internship at a law firm in Los Angeles, so I had to pack up their rooms!

The girls like the new house and have their own little wing with a hallway between their bedrooms. I hung our family portrait on one hallway wall, and the picture of Patrick playing the banjo on the other side. I can see it when I walk up the stairs, and Bruce is okay with the placement.

On Monday, July 15, I started my counseling practicum. Who knew so many wonderful things could happen at the same time?

ENTRY 80

THE DAY I MARRIED BATMAN – NOVEMBER 30, 2019

Bruce's middle name is Wayne so he *is* Batman. Bruce is probably tired of all the Batman references, but we had fun using them when planning the wedding. The wedding turned out exactly as planned, except for my one special request, but I will get to that later. I think I spent nearly two years planning my first wedding, and we pulled this one off in a few months! We picked Thanksgiving weekend, so of course it was a busy time. It was also the first big holiday since we moved into our house, so we decided to have Thanksgiving dinner at our home.

On Thanksgiving morning, Bruce's mom, Carrol, and his step-dad, Joe, arrived. This was the first time the girls and I had met them, so having a few days to get acquainted was nice. I also wanted them to meet some of my family so they weren't over-whelmed on the wedding day. We had a great visit!

The night before the wedding, Bruce stayed in a hotel. I was a bundle of nerves. I had planned to pack for our Minnie-moon at Disneyland, and I probably would have found other ways to stress myself out! I sat up talking with Carrol and Joe instead, and by the time I went to bed, I was completely relaxed.

The next day flew by, as I had my hair done by Gaby and Mia Castillo, and Sierra did my makeup. Finally, Cathy and I headed to the venue. Bruce picked up the girls after we left, and they arrived a little later.

When it was time to start, Matt escorted in my mother-in-law, Barbara, my dad escorted my stepmom, Kandra, Bruce escorted his mom, and Denny accompanied my mom. Then we had Sierra, Camille, and Bruce's youngest daughter, Bethany, walk in together, followed by the best man and matron of honor, Gavin and Cathy. I wanted the wedding to be unique, so I entered with the opening to Prince's "Let's Go Crazy" and walked down the aisle to "Here Comes the Sun" by the Beatles. I was thrilled to be walked down the aisle by my Pop, Andre teNyenhuis. Pop clarified that he was "presenting me," not giving me away!

My dad officiated and made sure it was memorable by reading an entire paragraph for the ring exchange and then asking Bruce to repeat it! Bruce and I wrote our vows. His vows included the promise to provide me with excellent health insurance, and I promised never to quiz him on my family's names.

At the reception, we were toasted by Gavin, Cathy, Denny, and Sierra. Denny managed to include the "Batman" theme and a lot of crowd participation in his toast. We had a great time at the reception, which ended too quickly.

Now, back to the one thing that went wrong. I thought I was doing a good thing hiring a charity bartender, but I was disappointed with their service. I requested two special drinks in advance, and they did not bring them! Anyone who knows me well can probably guess that one was Diet Pepsi. The other was Diet Mountain Dew for Bruce. So yeah, all in all, it was a perfect day! As we drove to our hotel I excitedly updated my Facebook profile to reflect my new name, with teNyenhuis as my middle name. I also changed my relationship status to "married to Bruce Black."

Bruce and me

Dad, Kandra, Joe, Carrol, Bruce, me,
Mom, Andre, Barbara

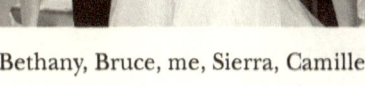

Bethany, Bruce, me, Sierra, Camille

The Bat Cake!

ENTRY 81

April 20 marked five years since my husband Patrick left for his early morning bike ride and never returned home. I try to write something each year to talk about my changes in perspective.

I took the day off, as I usually do. Patrick wouldn't want us to be sad all day, so we try to spend the day with loved ones and remember him.

Sierra and I started planning what we would do to remember him on Monday night. First up, *My Cousin Vinny*, one of our favorite movies to watch with Patrick. Sierra noted that watching the movie at the end of law school was interesting. She told me that numerous law professors had discussed the film, and she thought her dad would think that was cool.

Before I went to sleep, I found several pictures of us before we were married and one from our honeymoon to post. I recently reconnected with someone we both worked with, and reminiscing made me think of those days.

Mourning my first husband sometimes feels wrong, since I am happily married to Bruce. It can't be easy for him, but he gives me space and time to do it. And I know Patrick would want me to be happy.

He loved me completely, and knowing that has helped me in my grief. I've never second-guessed any decisions I have made since then.

Sierra and I had a lazy morning, and then we met Mom and Pop teNyenhuis for lunch. My brother, Denny, nieces Shayna and Katie, and Bruce joined us. We had fun reminiscing and just being together.

After lunch, we stopped by the liquor store and went to the cemetery, where Denny, Shayna, and Sierra had a drink with Patrick. We spent a lot of time walking around looking at headstones. As Denny put it, you appreciate all the time we had with him when you see the short life span of some people buried there.

After the cemetery, we went home, and Sierra went to hang out with her cousins (from both sides of the family) for a while. After Patrick died, our families merged. He would have liked that.

I spent some time alone with my thoughts, just remembering the good times. I looked through old pictures and laughed at the styles we embraced. After Sierra came home, we planned the rest of our evening. We decided to watch *Flight of the Conchords*. If you haven't watched the show, it's a sitcom about two musicians from New Zealand. They are corny, and it was precisely the type of show Patrick liked to watch. We also watched a few of their comedy routines on YouTube.

There was never a dull moment around Patrick. His dry sense of humor lifted our moods. If one of the girls was being overly dramatic, he would pat her on the arm and say, "There, there." This expression usually stopped any tears and created laughter. Later in the evening, we had a FaceTime call with Camille. We were all sad that she couldn't be home with us, but she was in her second week of a new job and couldn't take time off. She spent time telling us about her job, and we also reminisced a little. Mainly, we were just happy to end our day together.

I received messages via text and social media from friends and family throughout the day. Some of his fraternity brothers shared pictures, including one of him by his VW bus, which I had never seen before.

Patrick and his beloved VW bus

A perfect ending to the day was a message from another fraternity brother. He shared a picture via Facebook Messenger. The picture showed Patrick and four fraternity brothers "mooning" the photographer. I cracked up when I saw it and knew Patrick was smiling down at me. Of course, he would arrange to moon me!

ENTRY 82

I worried about Camille after Patrick died. She hadn't done a lot of visible grieving. I thought it might come up when she went away to school, and I was right. Camille went through struggles being away from her family and friends. And she missed her dad more than ever.

During her first year of college, she met a core group of girls who would become her roommates for the rest of college. She became involved in a Christian fellowship group that allowed her to demonstrate the leadership skills I always knew she had.

Camille also excelled in her classes. She did very well and graduated in June 2021 with honors, like her father and sister. Due to the pandemic, her graduation was a little subdued, but I was glad that Sierra and I could watch her walk across a stage in her cap and gown.

Camille took the Medical College Admission Test (MCAT) and scored extremely high. She is going to work at Community Regional Medical Center's rehab unit and take prerequisite classes for physician assistant school.

She has spent much time contemplating her future goals, and I am so happy she has found her purpose. I know her father is very proud.

We have moved forward with purpose and resilience. I made sure my daughters had love and support. I realized a dream I didn't even know I had and became a licensed counselor. We soaked in the love we knew Patrick had for us. I genuinely believe we were all able to achieve what we have because we wanted to make him proud. And I know that he is smiling down on us.

Camille and Sierra on Camille's graduation day

ENTRY 83

I 'll never forget Back to School Night when my oldest daughter, Sierra, was in the seventh grade. After her drama teacher finished her presentation, Patrick approached her and asked, "Can this class help her have less drama?"

He may have just wanted a chance to talk to the "hot" teacher (his words), but it is a funny memory. The drama class became the first step in Sierra's future.

Her time in the drama class was fun, and I enjoyed her portrayal of Cinderella's godmother in a comedic interpretation of fairy tales. I'm unsure if she had less drama, but she had a good time.

She switched directions in high school and joined the forensics team, participating in speech competitions and an occasional debate. Her coach, Mikendra McCoy, inspired her and helped her develop her skills and desire to pursue a career where she could use them.

Sierra made it to the state and national championships in high school. She also participated in the local mock trial competition, which sparked her interest in law school.

Over the years, Sierra had honed her debate skills, and she enjoyed arguing with her father. Sometimes, it seemed like they picked topics that would annoy each other. Occasionally, I had to tell them to calm down and agree to disagree. Finally, Patrick told her she should become a lawyer to argue with others.

Patrick and I were in awe of our children's success. We didn't feel we could be credited for it because we weren't doing anything special as parents. Our primary purpose was to love and enjoy spending time with our daughters. As simple as that was, it seemed to be enough.

Sierra was more of a challenge and she tended to panic when things weren't going her way. We had worried about whether she could make it alone in Long Beach. She exceeded my expectations.

Sierra moved back home for a gap year after graduating from Long Beach. She went with me to drop her sister off at UC Davis for her first year. She studied for and took the LSAT.

Her score was good enough to grant her a choice of law schools and scholarships. She chose Loyola Law School and received a scholarship covering nearly all her fees. Sierra had found her purpose. And with it, she demonstrated just how resilient she was.

Sierra continued to amaze me during law school. She kept her grades up even higher than I ever expected. I can't tell you how often she called to tell me she did horribly on a test. Then, she would call me back a few days later to say she got an A+. And one time, she got an A+*, which is apparently a thing.

During her second year, she made the moot court team, and for her final year, she moved up to the top moot court team at the school. In the fall, she participated in the regionals in her apartment via Zoom. She updated me with her usual undersell of "we probably won't do very well." Guess what? They *won* the tournament and qualified for the nationals!

The National Moot Court Championship is cosponsored by the New York City Bar and the American College of Trial Lawyers. It usually involves a trip to New York City with the excellent opportunity to network and sightsee. There was an unwelcome twist for the 71st Annual National Moot Court Championship. The pandemic forced the tournament to the Zoom platform.

Sierra and her teammate Jillian competed against 27 other teams. At the end of two rounds, they found themselves in the Top 16 as the top seed! For that round, Sierra finally told me there was a Zoom link. I could watch it, but I was not to forward it to anyone else. They won that round and the one after, putting them in the Top 4.

That night, I shared the news with my siblings and told them that the next round coincided with my lunch break, so I would be able to watch. They immediately started trying to get the link. Finally, we agreed that we could watch it together. I made them bring me lunch too!

My siblings and I were filled with pride. We all thought they had won the round, and we were right! Suddenly, my daughter was one step from the national championship! I had a full schedule of clients, but I managed to reschedule my last two clients for evening appointments, and I was able to watch.

The other team had strong competitors, and Sierra and Jillian were appearing as the respondent, which was their less-preferred side of the case. I reminded myself not to be disappointed if they didn't win. I didn't have to worry, they *won!!*

I wanted my daughters to be okay. They were more than okay. They demonstrated resilience and exceeded all of my expectations. Camille has many years ahead of her as she prepares to apply for graduate school. Sierra is a national champion, and she is listed on Wikipedia!

In May 2021, Sierra received her Juris Doctor with a Cum Laude distinction. She immediately began studying for the California Bar Exam. The exam was held during the last week of July, and a few days later, we celebrated her graduation in person!

California is one of the last states to release bar results, and she had to wait until November 12 at 6:00 p.m. The wait was agonizing. We were confident she would pass, but we had to wait for confirmation. Finally, at around 6:03 p.m., she emerged from her bedroom with a big smile. She passed!

Sierra hadn't wanted us to plan anything in case she didn't pass. But we threw together an impromptu gathering of aunts, uncles, and cousins. Everyone stopped by to toast Sierra and share in her joy.

Sierra decided to give a speech. I choked back tears as she told us about her journey. She said that when her dad died, she wasn't sure she could even go on, much less move forward and attend law school. And then, seeing the results of his court case, she was discouraged. She credited everyone in the room with supporting and helping her achieve everything. And she mentioned being proud that she could honor her father with this accomplishment.

Grief is a difficult journey. There is no right or wrong route to take. I'm glad Sierra found her purpose, and I feel Patrick is extremely proud of her. He is probably also bragging that it was all his idea!

I'm amazed that this all began in a drama class in seventh grade. When Patrick asked if the class would make her have less drama, the teacher laughed and said that it wouldn't take away the drama, but would help channel it into something more productive. And it has.

Dawan and Sierra

PART THREE

LIFE AS A WIDOW

ENTRY 84

GETTING THROUGH THE HOLIDAYS

I am more excited each year for Christmas than the first Christmas after Patrick died. During that first year, I didn't want to celebrate in all the ways I would have with Patrick. I made some *big* plans, which helped me get through. But I know what I did may not be feasible for everyone, so I will share what I did with some alternatives.

Change It Up

I started my escape from holidays on Father's Day 2016. Mother's Day came 18 days after Patrick died, and it was hard for me. So on Father's Day, I ran away. I took the girls and went to Universal Studios and Hollywood. I splurged a little on VIP passes. The next year we did Mother's Day at Disneyland. Even a day trip can be doable. If you can't face the usual holiday activities, change it up a bit. Go somewhere you usually wouldn't go. The novelty is distracting.

The girls and me at Disneyland on Mother's Day 2017

Take the Family Somewhere New

On the first Thanksgiving following Patrick's death, I rented a place big enough for 30 people, filled it with his family and mine, and we had a really good time. Going away together for a holiday was fantastic. We still missed him, but enjoyed being together and away from it all. We could have rented smaller houses or even hotel rooms. The important part is, we were at a place where memories would not haunt us, and we were together.

Turkey Trot on Thanksgiving morning

Front row: Olivia, Andrew, Ella, and Tina teNyenhuis

Back row: Matt teNyenhuis, Denise Campbell, Dawan Utecht,
Gabe teNyenhuis, Danell, Sierra, and Caitlin teNyenhuis

Don't Give Up on All of Your Traditions

Christmas was hard. We didn't want to deviate too much from
the norm. So we did some of our usual activities. And they were
made easier because the loss was acknowledged. The year before,
Patrick had started a new tradition of buying a Christmas tree
still tied up and then "unfurling" it at home. We were happy to
continue this tradition. And since he created it for us, it felt like
he was there! Luckily, our first Christmas without Patrick happened to be the year my family spent Christmas Eve at my sister's
house for one big sleepover. I was comforted by the familiar and
didn't wake up to a too-empty house on Christmas morning. We
also stuck with the Prandini tradition of gathering at a hall and
enjoying plates of ravioli together on Christmas Day. I'll admit
attending this event was hard. But I knew everyone there was

grieving, and not just for Patrick, since we had also lost his cousin, Barbara, and Zio Angelo. Cathy ended up joining me there, and that also helped.

Christmas 2016 – Pokémon Pajamas – Sierra, Aggie, and Camille

It's Okay Not to Be Okay

I don't remember what I did on New Year's Eve, but I think I stayed home and wanted to be alone. I wasn't ready to see other people get kisses at midnight. I wasn't moping and crying, but I didn't want to be around couples.

Do What is Best for You

My final advice is to do what is best for you and your family. If you're not the only one hurting, you may occasionally have to make hard choices to accommodate everyone. But outside of that circle, don't worry what others think. Everyone handles grief differently, and there's no right or wrong way.

ENTRY 85

DEAR NEWLY WIDOWED

Published in the *Fresno Bee*, April 20, 2018

I met a new widow yesterday. Our daughters went to school together, and I had heard of her husband's passing. We were both at a soccer game, so I introduced myself.

It's heartbreaking meeting people who have just lost a spouse. I know a bit about the journey they have ahead of them. I also know there is nothing anyone can do to take away the pain. I hugged her and gave her my phone number, which seemed inadequate. Here is what I would have liked to have told her.

> Dear newly widowed – I am so very sorry you are joining this club. None of us want to be here, but we try to stick together. I remember when I was in your place. I was in shock and didn't think I would ever recover. I wish that I could offer you some special words of comfort and magically take your pain away. I won't pretend to have that kind of power.
>
> Most people will not know what to do for you. Some of them will unintentionally add to your pain. I genuinely believe that most people have good intentions, but they just don't know what to do. When you think about it, it's surprising that death is still such a strange and uncomfortable topic. We will all die someday, but it is sad to think about losing someone. Most people like to think you just say goodbye and move on. Unlike those people, you and I know what it is like to lose the

person closest to you, the one who knew you like no other. Your journey is going to get harder before it gets better. I wish that weren't the case, but you are in shock right now. When that wears off, you will feel your loss even more. This is normal. Give yourself a break, and just allow some time to grieve. Don't let anyone give you rules or a timeframe. We all handle it differently, and there is no right or wrong way to grieve.

I believe our loved ones would want us to move forward and live the best life possible. It's hard to imagine doing that without them, but I'm trying to make my life meaningful as a tribute to the love we shared. You will find what works for you.

I can't promise that the pain will go away, but, for me at least, it has become more bearable. I still think of him daily, but it's usually a happy thought.

Remember that you are never alone. If you don't have family or close friends, there are various grief groups, online support groups, and many people who understand.

I'm so very sorry that we are meeting under these conditions. I promise to be here if you ever need me.

ENTRY 86

I CHOOSE HAPPY!

D uring graduate school I took a class called Spousal and Child Abuse, Crisis, and Trauma Counseling, which used the textbook *Crisis Assessment, Intervention, and Prevention* by Lisa Jackson-Cherry and Bradley Erford (2017). I was a little surprised that we didn't study the section on bereavement in that book. I think there is a certain expectation that everyone knows how to handle grief. I've learned that this is not the case. People have a wide range of reactions to death, and no one can prepare you for it.

When you are dealing with it, no one can tell you how to do it either. For the most part, you find your own way, hopefully with the help of friends and family.

I chose to read the section on bereavement on my own. I was interested in it because I've dealt with grief. Also, because I intended to be a crisis and trauma counselor, bereavement and grief would be part of that. Many people are familiar with the stages of death and dying. I think those stages apply to people facing a terminal diagnosis. They can also be applied to grief, but some don't fit well. In that textbook, I found a helpful four-stage guideline from J. William Worden's book *Grief Counseling and Grief Therapy: A Handbook for the Mental Health Practitioner* (1991), in which he lists four stages of grieving.

1. *Accept the loss* – These words initially seemed almost offensive to me. But it doesn't mean you agree with it, just that it happened. And it's not necessarily healthy to pretend nothing happened. Removing or avoiding reminders does not make it go away. I learned to make small changes that acknowledged the loss without being startling.

2. *Experience the pain* – Grief can be overwhelming! I tried to avoid the pain, but it always hit me when I least expected it. I finally learned to allow myself time to feel it and just let out the emotions. I haven't needed a good cry in a long time, but it helped when I needed it! I found that it helped me to know things that would trigger a good cry and to permit myself to let it all out.

3. *Adjust to an environment without the person* – Grieving families sometimes try to leave things "as is" to honor the deceased. For me, it helped to make minor changes a little at a time. My mind needed that to remind me he was gone, but I was still there. And I was okay. I didn't want to be stuck in one place; never moving forward would have been dreary. I'm not saying that's how everyone should do it, but it worked for me. Over the years, I was ready to make more significant changes. I didn't change everything at once. Baby steps.

4. *Reinvest emotional energy in other relationships* – This advice is essential. At first, it meant strengthening my connection with my family and close friends. Then it expanded to new friends, especially my fellow widows. Now it has progressed to a new relationship. I have a lot of love to give. And I know that Patrick would want me to be happy. I haven't moved on. I have moved forward.

I could spend my days wrapped up in memories of my years with Patrick. Remembering Patrick all day wouldn't be a horrible thing to do. I have a lot of great memories! But if that is all I did, I would spend a lot of time being sad and missing him. I don't want to be sad all the time. I choose happy!

And I think he would approve!

ENTRY 87

THE BOOK THAT GAVE ME STRENGTH TO SURVIVE

I don't remember when I first read Nancy Saltzman's memoir, *Radical Survivor: One Woman's Path through Life, Love, and Uncharted Tragedy.* Nancy published her book in 2014, and I think it must have been offered as a free e-book, which meant I could essentially rent it for free. I read it, but no longer had the book in my electronic library when Patrick died. I do remember it made a significant impression on me.

In September 1995, Nancy was happily married to the love of her life, Joel. She had survived breast cancer, and they felt fortunate. They spent a weekend in Las Vegas watching The Davis Cup with their sons, Adam, 13, and Seth, who turned 11 during the trip.

The family had flown separately from Colorado, since Joel and the boys had the opportunity to ride in a small plane with an acquaintance. Nancy took commercial flights, since she decided to go after Joel had made the travel plans for him and the boys.

The family had a great weekend together, and Nancy flew home a few hours before Joel and the boys planned to leave. In the evening, Nancy was waiting for them to return home when she received the call telling her the plane had not arrived when expected. Within a few hours, she received a second call confirming the plane crash.

There were no survivors.

There was no reason for me to connect with Nancy's story. I had no personal experience with tragedy. I was happily married with two children of my own. I think I identified with her as a mother. I couldn't imagine how she would go on if she lost her husband and children. I didn't think I would be strong enough to survive in a similar situation.

Right after Easter in 2016, Patrick, Sierra, and Camille took a day trip to California's Central Coast. The road on their drive home had 45 to 60 miles with limited cell phone coverage. I hadn't heard from them when I expected, and I remember briefly imagining the worst. And I knew if something did happen to them, my world would be shattered.

Legacy

Nancy has a large extended family who immediately surrounded her. She was an elementary school principal and quickly returned to work to keep herself busy and be around people.

Nancy was well-loved, and her community of friends and family strengthened her. Still, she went home alone every night and kept moving forward. Each day, Nancy got up and went to work.

She honored the memory of her husband and sons and did things to celebrate their lives. A memorial amphitheater was built at her elementary school to honor the family.

I believe the people who came forward to share what an impact her husband and sons had on their lives helped Nancy. Joel was well-known in the tennis community and owned a popular tennis shop. People she had never met came forward to share stories.

Each boy had classmates who reached out to Nancy to share memories. They all leaned on each other to survive.

My Loss

I thought of Nancy many times throughout the day of Patrick's death. I reminded myself she had lost much more than I had, and she survived. I knew I could too. Patrick was a physical therapist, and after he died, I heard from some of his patients who shared stories of the difference he had made in their lives. One even said she didn't think she would be walking if it weren't for him.

These were great stories my daughters enjoyed also.

Since then, the girls and I have leaned on each other to survive and thrive. We have each challenged ourselves to build meaningful lives, and we all view what we have chosen to do as a way to honor him.

Moving Forward

Nancy went on to survive a second bout with breast cancer. She continued her career in education and continues to touch the lives of others. She eventually remarried and is doing well.

I contacted Nancy on Facebook after Patrick died to tell her how much her book meant to me. She responded, and we became Facebook friends. I know she reads some of my updates because she will like or comment on them, and I do the same for hers.

Reach Out

You are fortunate if you haven't experienced the loss of an acquaintance who touched your life. If you have, or if you do in the future, make sure you take a few moments to reach out to their loved ones and share the impact they had on you. Nancy and I can tell you how much this thoughtfulness will mean to those left behind.

ENTRY 88

THE RED SHIRT

Have you ever watched a movie where someone has a kind of film loop running through their head? It's a real thing. Mine is Patrick, riding his bike, with a long-sleeved red shirt and the baggy bike shorts I bought him for Christmas (with hidden padding, so no one thought he was too serious about riding). He has an intense look because that's how he was when he was out riding. He viewed fitness as an obligation and usually looked serious when working out. He might have liked it a little, but he probably would argue with that.

Many people would think it's sad I have these images of how he would have looked right before it happened. And I guess maybe it *is* a little sad, but I'm used to it now. And yes, sometimes I let the film go forward a little and imagine what happened. I try not to do that too much because it is more challenging, but how little details matter is odd.

The day after Patrick's funeral, Mom and Pop (his parents) drove us to Porterville for Zio Angelo's funeral. I sat in the back with the girls on either side of me. We needed to go to be with everyone, and I was relieved we didn't have to be the focus anymore. While we were driving, Mom gave me a card she had been carrying around for Patrick and me. He had recently helped them put in a new mailbox, and I had done their taxes. The card was to thank us and included a gift card for dinner. She had been carrying it around since before he died. I knew she needed to give it to me, but I think it was hard for both of us. I choked up a little but vowed to keep it together for the girls.

Then my phone rang. The funeral home called to tell me they had a few personal effects—the clothing he was wearing that day. They thought I might want them thrown out. I had been trying to determine what he was wearing. I don't know why this was import-ant, but it just was. I thought it was the red shirt with black stripes down the sleeves, but I wasn't sure. I tried to ask without anyone in the car realizing what I was asking. I'm unsure how I did it, but they confirmed it was the shirt. I told them that someone would pick the items up. I got off the phone and struggled to hold it together. I spoke to Patrick in my head and begged him to help me keep it together, and I think he did.

We got to the church, and the rosary was first. This was good because I bowed my head as if praying, and sobbed. I think the girls were sitting by their cousins, and I had my teNyenhuis sisters-in-law with me, and they just surrounded me. After the rosary, there was a short break for viewing and visitation, and during this time, I moved and sat away from the girls. I knew their aunts would be with them, and I just needed to be away for a bit. I sat with Elisa, Marissa, and Livia (Prandini cousins), and I think I stopped crying, but it was nice to feel like I didn't have to hold it together. That great, big, beautiful family got me through that day. I love them all so much!

My sister picked up the clothing and packed it away somewhere. Probably, it should have been thrown out, but I just couldn't do it yet.

So I still occasionally have that little video playing.

Several years ago, I read a comment on a grief forum. A wid-ower described a suggestion from *With the End in Mind: Dying, Death, and Wisdom in an Age of Denial* by Kathryn Mannix that his friend recommended. According to the author's suggestion, the widower needed to tell the story of his wife's death more than 300 times to transform his experience of the loss.

> *Bereaved people, even those who have witnessed the apparently peaceful death of a loved one, often need to tell their story repeatedly, and that is an important part of transferring the experience they endured into a memory instead of reliving it like a parallel reality every time they think about it.*

Reading this quote over five years after I initially found it and three years after completing trauma training, I know more about how true this is. In 2023, I was certified in eye movement desensitization reprocessing (EMDR), an evidence-based treatment for PTSD and other conditions. Traumatic memories are stored differently than other memories. They are very uncomfortable, and many people push them aside and will go to great lengths to avoid reliving them. When I practice EMDR, I am helping my clients therapeutically process those memories, but many people never need that kind of treatment. The reasons vary, but I agree that talking about death can help normalize it, making it easier to recall without being overcome with the original emotions.

Now I know this intrusive thought of Patrick riding his bike in his red shirt is not causing me ongoing trauma. I have received treatment for parts of my grief journey that needed processing, but this was not one of them. It's not constant, and it's not horrific. It's just him riding. I still can't believe this happened. Over time, it has gotten easier. I don't cry very often, but it is still shocking every time I am reminded that he is gone.

We need to be more comfortable talking about death. We will all lose someone, and we will all die. It's okay to acknowledge that. Tell your story. Listen to mine. Each time, it will get a little easier.

ENTRY 89

TRIGGERS

I'm supposed to be in a good place. I'm happy, and I have a fantastic husband. I also apparently have some unresolved grief.

On January 26, 2020, when I saw the breaking news alert about Kobe Bryant, I immediately thought of my good friends Lisa Walthall and Diana Durham. They are both huge Lakers fans and have taken me to Lakers games. I imagined that it would hit them hard. I enjoy professional sports, but I don't follow them a lot. I ran downstairs to tell Bruce the news, and then I sat down in front of the TV and obsessively watched the news for hours. And I got sadder and sadder. Sierra texted Camille and me to say, "I love you." I asked if they had heard the news, and Sierra said that's why she had texted. We texted back and forth a bit about how awful it was, and then I continued watching the news.

I tend to be a news junkie when something terrible happens. I worried that Bruce would think I was obsessed, but honestly, I *was* obsessed! Who was in the helicopter with him? How many children did he have? Were they with him? At first, the news said there were five people. At that point, I thought he had three kids. If he happened to be the pilot of his helicopter, he might have been flying the whole family. So then I was agonizing over whether or not they had all been in there. As horrible as that would have been, it would have meant no one was left behind.

Then I found out he had four daughters, and I felt sick at the thought that possibly one family member was left behind. What if it was a kid? How do you come back from that?

After several hours, I started realizing that I had probably watched enough. I was going to turn off the TV, but I watched a news conference first. And they said there were nine people in the helicopter! Once again, I obsessed over the possible scenarios, each worse than the others. Finally, I turned off the TV, spent time with Bruce, and tried to feel better. By then, it was evening. I went to bed wondering why this was hitting me so hard.

Once in bed, I still couldn't sleep. I thought about Nancy Saltzman.

I checked Nancy's Facebook page, and she hadn't posted anything. But she had shared a post from Michele Neff Hernandez, who I recognized as the founder of Soaring Spirits International, a support group for widows and widowers. The message discussed wondering how Vanessa Bryant was coping and acknowledging that some of us have gone through similar losses.

After reading that, everything fell into place. Even though this tragedy was not the exact circumstance, it was close enough to trigger painful memories. I'm not alone; many of my fellow widows and others who have lost loved ones also felt incredibly sad.

I drove to work Monday wondering if I was fit to do counseling. I have an ethical duty to monitor my fitness to counsel. I felt okay, but I also continued to monitor myself. At one point, I talked to my coworker, Andrew Hernandez, and shared my feelings. He validated my feelings and reassured me. That night, I spoke more about my feelings, and Bruce thanked me for sharing and asked how he could help. Did I mention that he is wonderful?

As the week wore on, I wasn't feeling any better. I talked about it during supervision at work and decided I should probably go back to counseling myself. I'm realizing that there are certain parts of this journey that I have not let myself feel. It's easy to do. People told me I was doing it, and I didn't believe them. Sometimes, suppressing feelings is a survival mechanism, and I did what I needed to do. But I pushed a lot deep inside me, and now it needs to get out.

Last night I was at a low point, and I cuddled up with Bruce and told him the story of April 20, 2016. I thought I had already told him. I thought I talked about it all the time. But apparently, I mainly share happy memories. I shared all of the really painful ones and had a good cry. Bruce thanked me for sharing and I felt better after talking to him. It's comforting to know he is okay with listening to me talk about Patrick. It was a good start to a new journey I have to take. Since I'm a counselor now, I've decided this is a learning opportunity for me. I'm going to try a few different approaches, and I'm going to write more, since that helps me.

ENTRY 90

UNCLOGGING THE TOILET AND OTHER USEFUL SKILLS

Since marrying Bruce, I have realized I am falling into the state of learned helplessness I swore I would never fall into again. Bruce oversees the yard and anything electrical or electronic. Let's be clear: he takes care of everything. I like being taken care of, but a small part of me worries that I might forget what I've recently learned.

When Patrick died, I felt helpless in many ways. I was living in a 20-year-old house that was beginning to show signs of aging. We had a jacuzzi he was nursing along and a saltwater pool that tended to grow algae. There were also trees in need of pruning, rats living in one of them, and a beautiful yard Patrick spent hours caring for every week.

I had a lot of people willing to help me, and I appreciated that. Some of them offered their services without being asked. The neighbor's sons pulled my trash cans to the curb for months. I had a lot of other people who were willing to help and came by anytime I asked. But I hated to ask.

I probably didn't want a lot of people around helping. Being around people can be exhausting. Part of the reason was my life-long tendency to make sure everyone else was happy. I didn't want to make anyone sad. I preferred to grieve alone or with one or two people at a time. I also liked to try to take care of things myself.

I could have just hired professionals from the beginning, but doing anything, making any decision, was a chore. Tackling one thing at a time seemed to work best for me. My first order of business was the pool.

Summer came soon after Patrick died. I tried to hire a pool service, but I had large trees by the pool, and they seemed to drop leaves year-round. As a result, I had trouble finding someone willing to do the work. In the meantime, the pool was beginning to have a green tint.

We had a saltwater pool that needed chemicals to maintain a balance. I remembered that Patrick would take pool water in to be tested. And I was pretty sure I knew where he took it. So I headed to Clearwater Pool and Spa. I got there and told them I had no idea what I was doing, but I had brought pool water! They asked me how many gallons my pool had. How would I know that? Luckily, they found Patrick in the system, which gave them all the information they needed. They tested the water and sold me the chemicals.

The pool was soon sparkly clean! I had to return a few times, since it wasn't staying clean. Then they told me the filter probably had to be cleaned. I hired someone to do that the first time, but the filter kept losing pressure with all the leaves and algae and needed to be cleaned again. And I didn't want to pay $100 each time. I pulled out YouTube and taught myself how to clean it. Finally, the pool stayed clean!

Shortly after that, the girls and I spent a week on vacation. When we came back, the pool was looking green again. I headed back to Clearwater Pool and Spa with my usual water sample. I explained to the owner that my pool looked good until I went on vacation for a week. "You left your pool for a week during the summer? You can't do that!" he said. "What?! I did not sign up for a 'pool baby,'" I thought to myself.

Eventually, I had the trees trimmed and was able to hire a pool service. Someone else could take care of the pool!

The next issue was a clogged toilet. I knew how to use a plunger, but Patrick would never buy them. If a toilet backed up, he insisted on using a scary-looking tool called a toilet auger. The auger was a miniature toilet snake. I hated it because it was gross. To unclog the toilet, you inevitably got some of what was clogging the toilet on the auger and EWWW! I bought a plunger and vowed never to use the auger. Then a toilet got plugged up. The plunger didn't work. The drain cleaner didn't work. I got the auger out in desperation, watched a YouTube video, and immediately unclogged the toilet! I guess my husband wasn't just stubborn; he was brilliant too. A few years later, my neighbor's toilet got clogged, and I headed over with my auger and took care of it.

I finally hired a gardener, but couldn't figure out how to set the sprinkler timers. Patrick had them set, but there was a leak, and I needed to turn off that zone. My brother adjusted them a few times, and then I figured out I could order a smart sprinkler system with an app for my phone. We turned off the sprinklers for the winter, and I was going to have my brother install the system, but we kept forgetting. Eventually, I watched another YouTube video and installed it myself.

Two years into widowhood, and I felt pretty independent. I was proud of the tasks I had learned to do. And I used my story as a cautionary tale for my married friends. I told them to make sure they both knew how to handle the household tasks the other was in charge of.

I have learned a lot of hard lessons since becoming a widow. Although I eventually figured things out, there were many tears and pity parties before that happened. Mostly, I have learned that I am not helpless. I can get things taken care of around the house. I never had to before, but I figured it out when push came to shove. I think we can all do much more than we think. And now I feel more appreciative of Bruce's abilities while feeling competent too.

ENTRY 91

WRITING CAN RELIEVE YOUR EMOTIONAL PAIN

In the first few years after Patrick died, I would wake in the middle of the night and feel utterly alone. I knew I had a village of family and friends who were willing to talk to me at any time of day. However, it was hard to make those calls in the middle of the night. So I wrote. And I keep writing.

> *"The aim of art is to represent not the outward appearance of things, but their inward significance."*
> — Aristotle

When I was growing up, I developed a love of writing. I never had a diary, but I did like to journal or write short stories. Writing was especially helpful when sorting through feelings, such as a first kiss or a breakup.

When I met Patrick in 1986, we attended college in different cities. At the time, long-distance phone calls were expensive. His only phone was a shared telephone in the hallway of his dorm. The limited access to the phone made communication even more difficult.

My first cell phone was 10 years in the future, and neither of us had an email address or a computer. We had to rely on the U.S. Postal Service for most of our communication. As a result, I spent hours pouring out my feelings in letters to him, and Patrick did the same for me.

After we both graduated and got married, I did very little writing. I never really thought about it or felt the need to write. I just no longer needed to write down my feelings.

"In short, you have only your emotions to sell.
This is the experience of all writers."
— F. Scott Fitzgerald

After Patrick died, my friend Sonia (who is also a widow), gave me a journal. She told me that writing was therapeutic for her. I began writing in the journal, and then quickly transitioned to blogging.

I did most of my writing on my phone, mainly because I wrote late at night when I was having trouble sleeping. My phone was always nearby, and I could write until I couldn't keep my eyes open any longer. Writing helped clear my mind and enabled me to get much-needed sleep.

I didn't publish everything I wrote, but made it clear to my audience that I was writing to release my pain. I wouldn't leave the painful parts out to avoid making people uncomfortable. I wrote from my heart.

Over the years since Patrick's death, I have used my writing to document my pain, record memories, and celebrate accomplishments. Writing and sharing my words contributed to healing. My experiences while writing my blog also helped me decide to return to school to obtain a master's in professional clinical counseling.

While in school, I transitioned to academic writing. This writing type was more challenging and taught me how to research. It also contributed to healing by increasing my knowledge, providing a sense of accomplishment, and improving my writing skills.

I began my internship in July 2019 and graduated in April 2020. I wrote about those accomplishments. I also documented the disruptions caused by COVID-19, including my canceled graduation.

*"Writing is a form of therapy; sometimes I wonder how all those who
do not write, compose, or paint can manage to escape the madness,
melancholia, the panic and fear which is inherent
in a human situation."*
— Graham Greene, *Ways of Escape*

As a counselor, I encourage my clients to journal; many of them
bring their journals to sessions to share with me. I explain to them
that there are many reasons to journal. Journaling allows you to
document your progress. You can look back at entries from prior
months to see how your outlook has changed.

I also suggest my clients use writing to articulate unspoken
thoughts. Getting thoughts onto paper is essential when a client
wants to say something to someone who is no longer available
due to estrangement or death.

There are times when clients write these messages in anger.
Expressing anger in a relationship is not always advisable, and it's
not even possible in some instances, such as death. Translating
these thoughts into written words makes them tangible, something you can touch.

When clients have unresolved anger, I recommend they write
down their thoughts. Then they can symbolically destroy their
anger by crumbling the paper into a ball, tearing it into small
pieces, burning it, or even doing all three!

A teenage client became excited about the prospect of destroying
his anger. He quickly wrote a message and then tore it into small
pieces. His relief was immediate. I had joked about burning the
pieces, but gave him the disclaimer that he should use caution
because we live in California, and many parts of the state were
on fire.

In the next session, my client told me that he burned the pieces
safely in a barbecue. He was very proud, and genuinely felt
decreased anger. He planned to use the technique to write other
messages.

I am always working to expand my counseling skills and discover different areas of specialization. I don't currently practice a structured form of writing therapy. My knowledge comes from personal experience and is not part of my clinical practice. Based on the studies I have recently reviewed and the effects writing has on my clients, training in this type of treatment would be an excellent future investment.

Until then, I will continue my practice of using writing to improve my own emotions. And I will continue to encourage my clients to write.

ENTRY 92

TIME CAPSULE

"To live in hearts we leave behind is not to die."
— Thomas Campbell

There is no rule book for handling the belongings of your late spouse. I did not think I would be going through his things years later, but I've done it at my own pace.

When Bruce and I combined our households, moving was stressful. Luckily, we have an oversized garage with room for many boxes. We intended to do a little at a time, and then time passed.

I've had multiple boxes of Patrick's things that I was holding onto. I was planning to get them all together and then go through and discard anything meaningless. How do you decide what is meaningless? I decided to consolidate the mementos into one box and save it as a time capsule for the girls or their children to look through in the future.

One box was filled with items packed up in college, moved home, and possibly never touched again:

- A worn deck of playing cards with the University of the Pacific logo and a campus picture. I remember playing spades in Patrick's dorm room or apartment using these cards. The cards might not be played again, but they could still be picked up, and the holder could imagine their father, or possibly their grandfather, handling the same cards.

- A cup made of leather with the name "Pat" on it. I assume it was a high school art class project. The cup was filled with pennies. I could cash in the pennies for a few bucks. Or they could age in the time capsule, along with the Ziplock bag labeled "Rare Coins."
- A "Guest List" notebook that was used as a sign-in for his bachelor party. Some of the entries are illegible; most are nonsensical. I was smiling at the thought of Patrick with his high school friends and cousins. Damian reminded him that he knew me first. John did not mention that he dated me first.
- High school ID cards for each of his years at Hoover High School.
- A school picture and a picture of Patrick running for the Sierra Freshman High School cross-country team.
- A book of poems and short stories published in his senior year of high school with contributors, including a classmate who is now the CEO of Valley Children's Hospital and another, Everett O'Keefe, who owns a small publishing company (and is helping me publish this book). Patrick had several contributions, including one about his great-grandmother. Of course, they got his last name wrong!
- High school awards, including certificates and plaques. Possibly, I will add the yearbooks, but for now, they are on the bookshelf for easy access.
- Cassette tapes that are mostly useless now.
- A picture from his high school prom with his date, Heidi.
- A pair of dice.
- Physical therapy tools to measure range of motion and pain sensation. And needles and thread to do minor repairs while away from home.
- A Jiminy Cricket figurine.

- A butane lighter.
- An expanding tin cup for camping.
- A metal "Honor Carrier" cash box from his days delivering *The Fresno Bee*. Locked, but easy to open with a screwdriver. Inside are various items, including his high school valedictorian medal.
- Various other items that I will leave as surprises for the girls. I realize that many of these items could be tossed in the trash. I save them because they meant enough to him that he kept them. And I feel close to him as I look through them.

My favorite item is a souvenir keychain from Magic Mountain. If you look into it and hold it up to the light, you can see a picture of Patrick and me. I've always loved the picture and I'm amazed that I was able to take a semiclear picture of it with my phone.

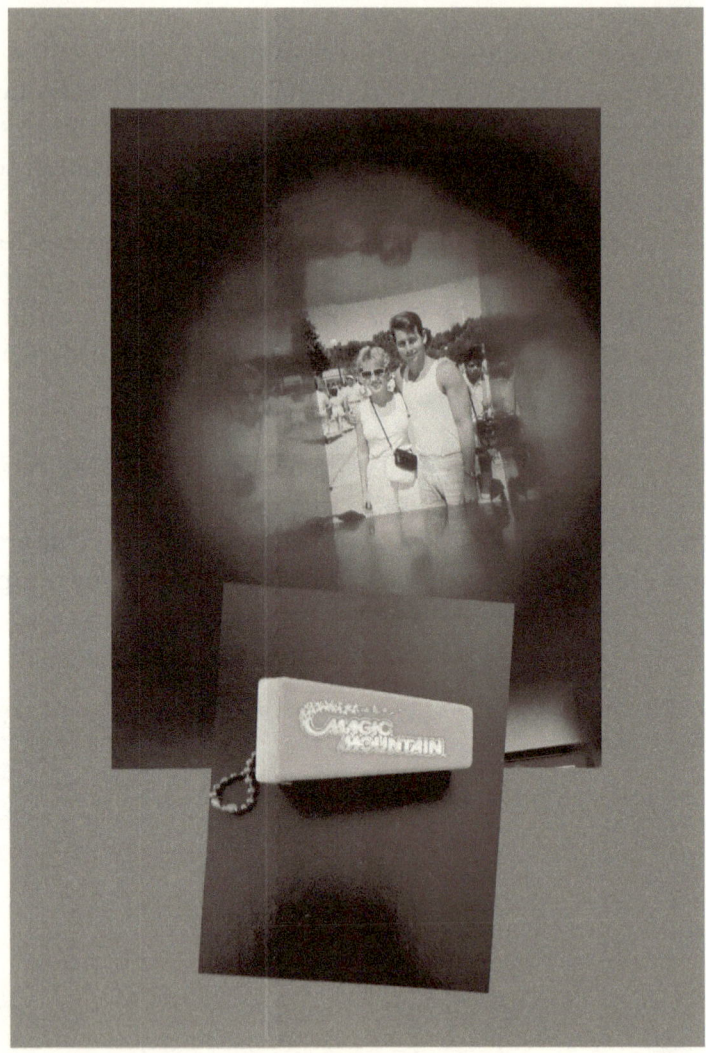

Picture from souvenir keychain with Patrick and me

I also know there are still more mementos in the garage. Someday, I will find them all and finish the time capsule. And when I do, I will look through everything again.

ENTRY 93

PERFECT WORDS OF COMFORT DO NOT EXIST

While I don't feel I have a tragic life, I have witnessed quite a few tragedies, starting during my childhood. Witnessing trauma doesn't make me an expert, but I think it has given me practice and the ability to remain calm. Sadly, I still haven't learned any magic words to make the tragedy easier.

Since I experienced the sudden, tragic loss of my husband, Patrick, in 2016, I've felt that I should know what to do when someone else is going through a similar experience. But I still feel very unprepared when trying to help someone experiencing tragedy. My best advice is to do and share, which I will explain shortly.

On January 12, 2022, I heard the shocking news that a local cyclist had been hit and killed while riding. Sadly, I knew the cyclist, Paul Moore, and his sister, Diana Durham, is a good friend.

Ironically, Paul was one of the few Fresno cyclists who had ridden with Patrick. He liked to tell the story of Patrick showing up on his "beater bike" and surprising Paul when he could actually keep up with him.

I texted Diana and told her how sorry I was. I was just honest and told her there were no words. I told her I felt like I should know what she needed and she shouldn't have to ask, but I asked her to let me know if I could do anything.

Then I just sat and had a good cry. I knew what was ahead for Paul's family, and there was nothing anyone could do about it. And this wasn't a new experience for Diana or myself.

Sonia and Kevin

On a Sunday morning in 2004, I received a phone call from my friend and former coworker, Sonia, who had transferred from Florida to Fresno. We had become close while working at Aetna. She lived in the foothills, around 30 minutes away, and had no family nearby.

When I answered the phone, I heard Sonia say, "I think Kevin's dead." Kevin was her husband. He was full of life, and they were deeply in love. Sonia spoke in a whisper, and she seemed to be in shock. I told her I would come to her house, then hung up.

As I drove up to Sonia's house, I called Diana. She had been our boss at Aetna, and I now consider her a close friend. I gave her the limited information I could get from Sonia, and she also agreed to head to her house.

While I drove, I thought about Sonia's stories about Kevin. They had so much in common and loved their life together! I could tell they were soul mates, and I couldn't imagine what Sonia was going through.

I don't remember every detail of that day, but I remember I didn't know what had happened to Kevin. As I drove up their long drive-way, I saw a small tractor had overturned. Emergency responders were gathered around, and I could tell there was a body. I kept going and pulled up to the house.

I forget what we said or did. Diana arrived right after I did, and we tried to be there for Sonia. I know we discussed the shock of the situation, and Sonia shared memories. I know I didn't have the perfect words for Sonia because perfect words don't exist in this situation. It was a difficult day, and this may sound strange, but I feel honored that Sonia asked me to be there with her.

Patrick

Years later, in 2016, both Sonia and Diana would support me when Patrick died. They would both visit and be there to listen. As I previously mentioned, when Sonia visited, she brought journals for the girls and me, and that is how I began writing about my grief. I eventually transitioned to writing publicly in my blog.

I've often thought that being with Sonia on her worst day prepared me for my own worst day. I can't put my finger on exactly what I learned, but the most important lesson was that Sonia kept living. Her life was never the same, but she moved forward and kept Kevin's memory alive. I'm grateful I had her, as she was someone who knew what I was going through.

I promised to explain what I meant by doing and sharing. I've often heard that, rather than ask what you can do for someone who is grieving, find a task and do it.

Doing

Figuring out what someone needs can be difficult. You want to be helpful but not intrusive. Helping might mean washing dishes, running errands, or taking out the trash. If you want to bring dinner, you could say, "Can I bring you dinner tonight or tomorrow night?"

For example, after Patrick died, his aunt, uncle, and cousin wanted to help with yard work. Rather than asking if I needed them to do the yard, they said, "We would like to help with yard work. Will Tuesday evening work for you?" I will always be grateful for the help they provided.

Sharing

When in doubt, just listening is good. Let them tell their story.

The day Patrick died, and many times since then, people reached out to share stories. I had never heard many of these stories, such as the ones from patients who reached out to tell me how much his treatment had helped them.

There were also stories I had heard before but forgotten. Some of the best stories involved Patrick's quirky sense of humor. These types of stories helped lift our mood, which was a blessing.

Some memories were shared in person, some on social media, and others in cards and letters. In addition, Patrick's employer left a few journals out and allowed patients and coworkers to add their condolences. These pages also included great stories.

I reread the stories from time to time. I am happy there is a written record of Patrick's life, and I will always cherish the memories.

Paul's family will have a written record too. Reading the many tributes on his Facebook page from past students and fellow cyclists clarifies how special he was. I wish I had been able to spend more time with him. I'm devastated that his family, including Diana, his wife, Marcia, son, Andrew, and many others, are experiencing his loss. But I'm happy they are surrounded by love and so many stories. I know this will mean a lot to them.

ENTRY 94

HOW I DID GRIEF ON MY OWN TERMS

G rief is a strange experience. Sometimes you know it's coming, and it's a long, drawn-out process. Grief can also visit you in surprising, shocking ways. No matter how grief happens, life rarely prepares us for it.

Over seven years into my grief journey, I can reflect on a few things that made it easier to move forward. I'm not writing a manual, because every journey is different. Instead, I will share what worked well for me.

The Concept of Tragedy

I used to think that real tragedies only happened to other people. Sure, I had experienced tragedies. I had front-row seats for several of them. But none of them changed the course of my life.

I'm sure that everyone has nightmares about awful things happening. I know I did. One involved my husband and daughters being in a horrible accident and not surviving. Even imagining something like that terrified me.

I was 100 percent certain that if something awful happened to one of my immediate family members, I would fall to pieces. If I lost them all, I couldn't move forward. I wasn't a strong person. Life was about to prove me wrong.

My Tragedy

Several weeks after one particularly awful bad dream, my real nightmare began when Patrick was hit and killed. As the day passed, family and friends filled my house, and I realized I wasn't alone.

Terror and Numbness

As a counselor, I have learned a lot about trauma. We all have a window of tolerance. We can handle periods of hyperarousal (pain, terror, panic) above our window of tolerance. But if we spend too much time in hyperarousal, we can fall below the window of tolerance into hypoarousal (numb, collapsed, shut down).

To function normally, we need to spend most of our time in the window of tolerance. All three states are necessary, and I am incredibly grateful for hypoarousal, as it got me through the first few weeks. I survived the funeral planning, the viewing, and the actual funeral because I was numb. The shock protected me and kept me functioning.

Gratitude

I will always say gratitude was the biggest reason I kept moving forward. I was so grateful for everyone who reached out and lifted us during that time. Someone was always there to help make essential decisions, bring meals, clean up, and support us.

Paying that forward became a blueprint for my life. I wanted to ensure that I honored that spirit of giving and lived a life Patrick would be proud of. And I wanted to focus on what I still had: two incredible daughters I love dearly.

I am especially grateful for my siblings.
At my nephew Dustin's wedding, September 2017.
Denny, Dawan, Denise, and me.

Routine

Sticking to or developing a new routine is an important step. I used the simple act of walking to the mailbox and getting the mail daily as a reminder that I was still living my life.

The rest of my routine took longer to develop, but I made sure that I regularly planned my schedule so I wouldn't just have empty days to get lost in my thoughts. I encourage my clients to stick to a routine when they are going through difficult times.

Writing

I started journaling and then blogging about what happened. I didn't want to forget anything people said or did for me. And talking about my grief felt healing. I started a blog, named it *My Life After Patrick*, and wrote a minute-by-minute account of the day he died, including the messages I received.

Along the way, I discovered that my writing was helping other grieving people. Getting supportive feedback encouraged me to continue, and eventually I found that I wasn't always writing about grief. My writing was and is a very healing activity for me.

Changing My Environment

After a few months had passed, I slowly began making small changes at home. As strange as it may sound, I needed physical reminders that Patrick was gone. I wanted them to be subtle so they wouldn't cause intense grief.

Clearing out his clothing was painful, but it was better than having the daily reminder each time I went into the closet.

I reorganized the kitchen cabinets and rearranged their contents. Although subtle, the change symbolized that life was different, yet we were okay.

Significant Days

When you're grieving, there are many significant days that you have to face. In addition to the usual holidays, there are birthdays, anniversaries, and the date of death.

The first holiday after Patrick's death was Mother's Day. I didn't think this would be a hard day, and I wasn't prepared when it was. From that moment forward, I approached holidays on my own terms.

For Father's Day, the girls and I left town and spent a few days in Hollywood. We visited the Getty Museum, the Walk of Fame, and Universal Studios.

We did many other special things, including trips to Catalina Island, the beach, and Hawaii. Patrick left us in a good position, and we had the means to do things we had never done before. These options are not available to everyone, but anyone can start new traditions.

For Patrick's birthday and the anniversary of his death, which are one week apart, we try to go to places he loved and do things he would enjoy. Our remembrances have involved going to places such as the beach or lake, and we try to be together whenever possible.

We kept some holiday traditions, and we were eventually able to celebrate holidays as we had in the past, minus Patrick.

Purpose

Finding purpose is essential to mental health. During my education and training, I learned to work with clients to identify activities that give them purpose. Working, volunteering, or pursuing higher education are all ways to find a sense of purpose.

I took some time off work and then was able to take early retirement after Patrick died. I enrolled in a graduate program and earned my master's in professional clinical counseling. In late 2023, I became a licensed professional clinical counselor.

At my graduation from Grand Canyon University –
Camille, me, Sierra

As a counselor, my education and experience have reinforced many lessons I learned during my grief journey. I now regularly prescribe journaling to aid in healing. I also use my experience to suggest other activities for grief and mental health in general.

I have found helpful information about navigating grief at soaringspirits.org and optionb.org. Both sites provide access to online support groups.

Keep Moving Forward

The best advice I can give anyone is to keep moving forward. Don't be afraid to have new experiences. Three and a half years after Patrick died, I remarried and am experiencing a new chapter in my life. Meeting and marrying Bruce happened because I was willing to move forward.

There is no magic formula to take the pain away. And no one wants to lose the memories of good times. Find a way to embrace your new life. Do grief on your own terms!

APPENDIX

Patrick's Obituary

Patrick John teNyenhuis, April 13, 1967–April 20, 2016

The banjo fell silent in the early morning hours of Wednesday, April 20, 2016 when our beloved son, husband, father, brother and friend Patrick John teNyenhuis left for his regular bicycle ride and never returned.

Patrick was born in Fresno on April 13, 1967 to Barbara and Andre teNyenhuis. His mother was a Prandini, giving him two large families from birth, Dutch and Italian ancestry, devastating good looks and a mind that never stopped asking how and why things worked the way they did.

Patrick was valedictorian of his class at Hoover High School and went on to graduate from both the University of Pacific and Chapman College, where he was awarded a Master's Degree in Physical Therapy. He practiced at the Veterans Hospital in Fresno and later became a clinical manager at San Joaquin Valley Rehabilitation.

In 1992 Patrick married the love of his life, Danell Boyles, and together they raised two daughters, Sierra Elizabeth and Camille Barbara. Patrick achieved much in life but talked only of his pride for his girls.

At his side throughout life were his brothers and sister and their spouses—Daniel and his wife Amy, Gabriel and his wife Jennifer,

Matthew and his wife Tina, and Dina and her husband Jeff. Patrick became brother to Danell's siblings, Denise, Dawan and Tom Utecht, Wes Campbell and Denny, and was an amazing Zio to dozens of nieces and nephews. Danell's parents, Dennis and Kandra, and Diane and Ernie, claimed Patrick as their own.

His favorite saying was that Joe Reinartz was his only friend.

Patrick was passionate and dedicated in everything, from helping thousands of patients recover from injury, to teaching himself how to play the banjo and brew beer from scratch. He exercised eight times a week, ran several marathons while wondering why people would pay to run, and was amused that he could keep up with other cyclists on his trusty mountain bike.

Patrick enjoyed fishing, though it was the one thing he did that he didn't excel at. He was clever and witty, though sometimes he was the only one who understood his point. Most of the time, he was the subject of his own jokes. He was a member of the Kings River Bluegrass Association, Divine Mercy Catholic Church, and Fresno Floorball Club.

Patrick was preceded in death by his grandparents, Antonio and Teresa Prandini, and John, Tecla and Elsie teNyenhuis.

His friends and family can still hear his voice singing both alone and with his bandmates, often sipping a beer he brewed himself. His song will never end. He will welcome us all to heaven with music and his smile.

Visitation will be held at Whitehurst, Sullivan, Burns and Blair Funeral Home on Tuesday, April 26, 2016 from 4:00 p.m. to 7:00 p.m., followed by Recitation of the Holy Rosary at 7:00 p.m.

A Mass of Christian Burial will be held at St. Paul Newman Center in Fresno on Wednesday, April 27, 2016 at 10:00 a.m.

In lieu of flowers the family requests a donation to the Divine Mercy Charity building fund in his name.

Eulogy

Written by Denny Boyles and read by John Prandini

Patrick liked to talk . . . about everything. He once talked for 20 minutes about why the core of a head of lettuce was the best part.

And Patrick would talk to anyone . . . he even enjoyed conversing with annoying telemarketers and would cheerfully ask them for their home phone numbers so that he could interrupt their dinner with their family like they were interrupting his.

Patrick had opinions . . . about everything. In fact, he had an opinion that he didn't agree with funerals. Somewhere above us right now, Patrick is telling whoever will listen that he never wanted a funeral and that he is not here, so why would we all be here talking about him?

On that point, Patrick is wrong. He is here with us. He is next to his parents, trying to comfort them. He is standing behind his sister and brothers holding them up. He is with Danell, telling her that he has taken care of her. And most of all, he is with Sierra and Camille, whispering that he will never leave their hearts.

Patrick's family is so very grateful to all of you here today and everyone who has surrounded us in love for this past week.

Today we remember the end of Patrick's journey on earth, but not the end of his story. For my part, today, I'm going to help us celebrate him, as best I can, with love and laughter.

On that note, I think it's worth sharing that Patrick could fit his entire cell phone into his mouth. Many of us here today can swear to it, and many of us walked away whenever the latest demonstration started. Of course, due to his aversion to technology and smartphones, the phone was a pretty small one.

Patrick's life story is, of course, set to music. Banjo music with a bluegrass theme, played near a Volkswagen bus topped by a canoe and filled with a lifetime of memories.

The chorus of the song is his family. That song will never end.

Patrick was the second child of five to his parents, Barbara and Andre. Pat was a lot like his dad. Handsome and with a love of conversation and, of course, his frugality. Patrick used to tell the story of how his parents were so thrifty that they used to wash their paper plates! And Pat adored his sweet and precious Mom, Barbara. She instilled a love of God in him, which sustained him throughout his life. He always looked up to his parents and their strong marriage as an example for his life.

From his youth, Patrick lived life in his own way. In high school, Pat had a tacky red hat with yellow flowers in a Hawaiian pattern that he wore *all the time,* and everywhere he went. It drove his siblings crazy. Though they routinely hid the hat from Pat, he always managed to find it, put it back on, and continue wearing it, annoying them all.

Pat once said that the reason his Mom and Pop had Matt was because they couldn't afford any more toys for their kids, and they could all play with Matt instead. Matt remained his favorite toy.

Growing up, according to Patrick's brother Dan, the teNyenhuis kids were each other's best friends. The bond between Patrick, Daniel, Gabriel, Dina, and Matthew is a testament to their parents. The Bible teaches us all to love our brother, and Patrick lived those words throughout his life, always in his own unique way.

The bonds Patrick formed with his siblings strengthened throughout his life. From pillow fights to running marathons to fishing and hiking, Patrick and his siblings and their spouses, Amy, Jen, Jeff, and Tina, shared so many wonderful memories.

Dan and Patrick shared a relationship that time and distance couldn't change. A family photo album from Dan's days as a Marine pilot in Hawaii shows Patrick smiling in pride next to his brother, sitting in a helicopter cockpit, or just being together. Amy met Danell, Patrick, and other members of the family before she met Dan. When Dan and Amy got married, Patrick welcomed her into the family by dancing circles around her, making crazy eyes, and pointing at random. Amy, you were warned early about life with Patrick . . . .

Gabriel and Dan share a passion for running, so Patrick ran. Then Matthew joined in, and the brothers and Dina logged many miles together, using the runs as a way to reconnect after long separations. There was always one brother who wanted a faster pace and the others running to catch up and call him an idiot.

Gabriel urged Patrick to run a marathon, so of course, he developed his own training plan and worked hard to qualify for the Boston Marathon, a milestone many train for. Patrick never planned to travel to Boston to run, however, because he didn't understand going so far for something he could do in his own neighborhood.

When Gabriel and Jen married, Patrick gained a lifetime supporter in Jen. She is that rare person who "got" Patrick and knew that nothing he said or did was done in harm. To Jen, Patrick was a superhero, a larger-than-life brother, father, and son who brightened rooms and made her husband smile.

Dina and Patrick shared a love of the outdoors. Dina brought Jeff into Patrick's life, giving him a fishing buddy and another brother. Together they relished time in the mountains, hiking, camping, fishing, or just drinking beer. Dina also shared her son with Patrick, naming him godfather to Desmond and forever bonding them together.

Matthew and Patrick shared a passion for brewing beer, which Matthew started and then watched as his meticulous brother overtook him on note-taking, if not on the quality of beer. Patrick left a batch of beer brewing for Matthew to finish but, of course, hid the notes.

If Patrick was a superhero to Jen, Tina was his kryptonite. For years she met his challenges head-on, keeping him honest. Patrick would always talk about women in math and women in science, likely just to bother Tina.

When challenged by Patrick to name a woman scientist other than Marie Curie, Tina found a book on women in science that immediately caught his interest. Not that he would ever concede a point. Despite their debates, Tina loved Patrick enough to share Ella with him, naming Patrick as her Godfather.

Danell's family wasn't spared from any aspect of Patrick either, something all of them will treasure. The first time Pat met Danell's family was at a party at Danell's Mom's house while her Mom was away. Danell had explained to Pat that she had one sister, Dawan, who was cool, and her brother, Denny, was cool, but the older sister, Denise, was a little uptight and might not be ok with the party. As it turned out, Denise's husband, Wes, ended the party in a tree, and Denise ended up at the bottom of the stairs, which she had ridden down on a piece of cardboard and put a hole in the wall. (Which their Dad had to come fix before Mom returned.)

Needless to say, this was just the beginning of many fun memories. New Year's parties and air guitar, Fourth of July parties with pool, barbecues, and fireworks (sometimes danger was involved!), beach campouts and family birthdays, and pajama Christmases.

Danell's parents, Dennis and Diane, and their spouses, Kandra and Ernie, could not have picked a better husband for their daughter and father for their grandchildren.

Denise and Dawan would have loved Patrick simply for the way he loved their sister, but loving Patrick was never simple or small, and for three decades, they built memories that will carry them forever.

Wes and Patrick formed an epic comedy team that frightened waiters and waitresses from Fresno to Pismo. Tom and Patrick held many deep conversations over pipes and cigars, and Patrick became Tom's brother in a way that will never cease. Scott and Patrick shared a love of music and floorball.

Denny's relationship with Patrick evolved from a young child chasing around an older brother to friends who shared beer and stories over backyard haircuts, Thanksgiving barbecue sessions, and banjo concerts.

All of the nieces and nephews remember Zio Pat as a quirky, fun uncle who sang goofy songs and created memorable sound effects for the annual reading of *The Night Before Christmas* and for his and Danell's great pool parties.

Patrick and Danell met in the summer of 1986 when they were both in their late teens. Danell was working for me, and she remembers the first moment she saw him. She knew a relative of mine was going to work there for the summer, and she just thought it would be an older relative. When she saw Patrick, she could not believe how handsome he was. They used to bring their lunches and then change into their bathing suits (which was a bikini for Danell) and go lay out by the pool for their lunch. That was the beginning of their love affair.

Patrick was quite the romantic and wooed Danell with passionate verse and extravagant gestures. They were known for their creative and elaborate Halloween costumes, always cleverly coordinated, sometimes in unexpected ways. Like the year they went as a slice of pizza and a Domino's "Noid," another year as Wayne and Garth, or the year they were Oscar and Emmy. They dated for 6 years before they got married. When they planned to marry, Patrick was adamant that parenthood was not in his future. Danell blithely assured us that Patrick would change his mind. Then, after a few years, Danell was pregnant, and her resolve was tested. And, of course, she was right. Patrick was instantly smitten and immediately fell in love with Sierra and, then, Camille. Once married, Patrick's whole purpose in life was to provide for Danell and, eventually, his girls. Everyone who knew him knew about his wife and his girls. They were all the loves of his life, and he was theirs. He loved them unconditionally, although not always conventionally. He took the girls on shopping trips to thrift shops, which he turned into contests for who could find the coolest bargain. He devotedly coached their sports teams and was their biggest fan at soccer matches and forensic debates. He made them order Port of Sub sandwiches using his frequent buyer card, which he had registered under the name Zoltar Sandwich. Camille insists that she is Zoltar!

He and Danell proudly took Sierra to Long Beach to go to college and, then, cried all the way home. He used to say that Sierra was the only vegetarian he knew who didn't like vegetables. Camille was his sidekick—fishing, canoeing, and hanging out. This past year, Camille's Varsity Soccer Team had an outstanding year and won the Valley Championship. Patrick was one of the proudest father's out there, attending almost every game.

He shared a special bond with both of his girls. He was proud of his teNyenhuis and Prandini heritage. He once told the girls that they were ¼ Italian, ¼ Dutch, ¼ Redneck, and ¼ Hillbilly. Danell's family didn't mind because it was mostly true! When Danell and Pat joined together, their families also formed a bond, which was strengthened through marriages, births, family holidays, and, now, death. That bond will never break.

A few months ago, Sierra and her Aunt Denise decided to surprise her mom and dad with a visit home. They were both so happy to see her, and Patrick told Danell that he had been having an especially hard week, but having Sierra home from college just made everything better. A week before his death, Danell and the girls took him to the Paul McCartney concert for his 49th birthday. Patrick told Sierra that the best present he got, even though he was thrilled about the concert, was having her home with him and their family together for his birthday. The girls are so grateful for those memories of their "one of a kind" Dad. While devastated, they know their father would hate seeing them sad and would want them to remember the funny things, the good times, and, most of all, to laugh. And Danell, his lover, his friend, and the foil for his dry humor and eccentric wit, has amazed us all. We have marveled at her strength through this difficult time. And admired her ability to remind us of his humor and his quirkiness and how he would want us to remember him. He dearly loved her, and she adored him and always will.

Patrick was an incredibly hard worker and persistent in all of his endeavors, whether it was yard work, attending to the pool, brewing beer, working, or his music. He liked to say that he only had one friend, Joe, but I'm pretty sure a lot of you here today would dispute that. While you might have to get used to his sarcasm and wit, there was a lot to love about him.

Pat touched countless patients' lives in his work as a physical therapist at the VA and San Joaquin Valley Rehabilitation Hospital. Some of them have shared the impact he had on their quality of life and their appreciation for that, which means so much to Danell and the girls.

Patrick also made many friends over the years, playing floorball. He was a fierce competitor, even against his nephew, Connor, and was known for doing 'whatever it takes' to win.

Banjo playing was a huge passion for Patrick. For years, he played in various bluegrass associations, including Saturday night jam sessions, Rodeo parades, and more. In the last few years, his love was his work with Steam Donkeys and his bandmates, Abdul and Mike. He wrote, played, sang, and truly shined, doing what he loved. Shannon could have done without some of the all-nighters, but the joy they all had playing together made it worthwhile.

And Patrick enjoyed riding his bike. In his usual Pat style, he was particularly proud of his 'anti-cycling culture' beat-up mountain bike and how he could out-cycle the thousand-dollar bikes.

There have been so many "God Moments" that have happened over the last year, especially since Patrick went to Heaven. Last year the teNyenhuis family was blessed with a 50th Anniversary Party for Mom and Pop teNyenhuis, where the entire family spent a week in Cayucos and got to enjoy each other. Also, there was a surprise 75th Birthday Party in the fall for Danell's dad, Dennis, where they had a huge turnout, and many people got to share more special memories with Patrick. We are so grateful for those times.

At Christmas last year, Danell bought Patrick a laptop. His first response was, "You bought me a laptop? Why on earth would you do such a thing?" to which Danell replied, without missing a beat, "You're Welcome." Because of that laptop, we now have the blessing of many videos of Patrick playing his banjo and singing songs, which we will treasure forever.

Patrick liked to be alone sometimes, but even in Heaven, no teNyenhuis or Prandini is ever truly alone. Patrick's uncle, Zio Angelo, passed away the day after Patrick. Some of us were wondering if the stress of Pat's death may have been too much for Zio Angelo, and that's why he passed so suddenly. Then we realized that Zio Angelo just did not want Patrick to go to heaven alone. We can see Zio Angelo smoking his pipe and steering his Corvette with Pat riding in the passenger seat, playing his banjo as they drive into heaven together.

Pat was adamantly against a memorial service. One of the reasons we are holding this service is to get back at him for all the jokes he pulled on all of us. A running gag between the siblings revolved around bottles of horrible beer they would trick each other into drinking. Once you were "it," you were obligated to pass the same beer on to someone else. One last prank is that Patrick was "it" this one last time, so hopefully, Heaven won't mind some pretty bad Cranberry Lambic.

I truly could go on and on with memories and stories of Patrick. And, I'm sure if Patrick had his way, I would. It would be very fitting, and the ultimate Patrick joke, to keep you here until midnight with memories of him. But I will leave you with this . . .

In the year 2000, Patrick decided to rebrand himself, saying that he was an adult and asking everyone to call him Patrick instead of Pat. To this day, Dan refuses because he is convinced it was Patrick's ultimate joke, played out for years.

For days, we've all hoped this, too, could be one of his jokes, the ultimate "gotcha" with a punchline that hasn't yet come. You got us, Patrick. We will never forget you, bud. Godspeed!

Statements Read in Court

February 16, 2017
The statement read by Denny

Your honor, I want to thank you for the opportunity to address the court. I'd like to start by reading a note from Daniel teNyenhuis, Patrick's brother, who cannot be here today. Dan is a retired United States Marine who still works to keep our nation safe. While we are in court for the sentencing of the man who caused his brother's death, Dan is at work defending us.

These are Dan's words –

> Patrick John teNyenhuis was my first friend and will always be my friend. I knew Pat before I knew anyone else. I spent my formative years with him. He significantly contributed to my personality and character. I owe much of my success to his influence. Yes, Patrick John teNyenhuis did live a blessed life. Pat deserved every blessing he received, including his three girls, Danell, Sierra, and Camille. Pat earned his other blessings through hard work and dedication, including his career as an expert Physical Therapist, where he routinely helped others in need. Patrick John teNyenhuis was a COMPLETE man in mind, body, and spirit, from his music and career to his health and physical fitness, to his family and faith. During his life, Patrick John teNyenhuis met people from all walks of life through his profession and his hobbies. Pat could talk with crowds and keep his virtue; he could walk with kings without losing his common touch. The world is a lesser place without the skills, music, and wit of Patrick John teNyenhuis.
>
> We all miss him.
>
> –Daniel Joseph teNyenhuis

I can't do a better job than Dan to describe Pat or the impact his life had on everyone around him. Before I sit down, though, I want to talk about the impact his death had and the actions that brought us all here today.

It's important that everyone in this room understands that we are not here by accident. Recently, following a court appearance, a member of the defendant's family told us that they were praying for us, but it was an accident. That is a lie.

Pat's death was not an accident. He died because of the irresponsible, selfish, and illegal actions of the defendant.

The defendant chose to buy an illegal drug.

The defendant chose to take that illegal drug. The defendant chose to get behind the wheel of a car and drive while under the influence of that drug and the sleep deprivation that resulted from its use. Whether it was intentional or not, the defendant then hit and killed Patrick. No logical person argues these facts.

Where logic still fails us all is the lack of accountability being shown here and the total lack of justice.

The defendant will be back with his friends and family within a year, while Patrick is gone forever from our lives.

Neither are things we can change. We have to try and accept them and choose to honor Pat's legacy rather than live our lives filled with anger over the unimaginably deep and painful hole he left behind.

We will spend the rest of our lives following Patrick's examples.

When this legal process started, many of us hoped that the defendant would be accountable for his actions and would take responsibility. As we learned more about his long criminal history, we were forced to give up that hope.

On April 20 of last year, the defendant forever changed the lives of our family and his own. The only hope I have left for some positive outcome from this terrible crime is that it is not too late for everyone in this courtroom to learn from a better example. For that hope, I offer the memory of Patrick.

Patrick was a man who loved God and his family. Patrick was a man who worked hard every day of his life. Patrick was a man who worked for everything he achieved in life and always shared what he had with those in need. Patrick was a man who often worked six days a week to provide a better life for his wife and children. Patrick was a man who had dreams and worked hard to achieve them. Patrick was a man who touched the lives of everyone he met. Patrick was a man who accepted the blame when he made mistakes and did everything he could to do better.

Patrick was a man.

Today I asked the court to do all it can to encourage the defendant to be a man from this day forward. To be a man and accept the terrible results of his crime. To be a man and work hard to change his life so that this awful scene is not repeated. To be a man and work hard to give his children a better example. To be a man.

Your honor, I thank you.

My Statement

My name is Danell teNyenhuis. For the last 24 years, I was Patrick's wife. Our marriage began in 1992 and ended on April 20th, 2016, when you took his life.

I am not a vindictive person. I know very little about you. I know you are a father, and I know that you made a series of poor choices that resulted in Patrick's death.

There is no punishment that will make up for the loss my daughters and I have suffered due to your choices. Unfortunately, our legal system was unable to find a way to adequately hold you accountable. So you will do your time and then have the rest of your life ahead of you.

What will you do with the rest of your life?

Let me tell you how Patrick lived his life. He was an amazing husband! We were truly partners in life. He helped with everything, including doing the grocery shopping and most of the cooking. He also found time to make me feel special and loved. He made all of my dreams come true. He was a wonderful father to our daughters, Sierra and Camille. His daughters were his pride and joy! When they were infants, he would get up with them at night, change their diapers, and then bring them to me to nurse. When they began eating solid foods, he made all their baby food from scratch. He attended sporting events, helped with science projects, and truly enjoyed spending time with them. They are beyond devastated by his loss. In the next year, one will graduate from high school and one from college.

Someday they will get married and have children, and he will miss these important milestones.

Patrick was an excellent physical therapist. I know because he helped me rehabilitate after hip surgery. I also know due to the numerous patients who have reached out to me since his death. Here is just one of the many stories that have been shared.

"In 2009 I had a surgery, which resulted in damage to my femoral nerve. Patrick became my physical therapist for an entire year, three times per week, as he persisted in trying to figure out the best therapy routine and exercise regime to help my femoral nerve regenerate and function. He did not know if the nerve was severed, crushed, stretched, or who knows what, but he was relentless in the challenge to help me be able to use my right leg again. I developed the greatest respect for him, his physical therapy skills, his tenacity and determination to take on the challenge and master the results successfully for me, as well as for his professional skills and efforts. The therapy was successful because of his training, perseverance, and knowledge. I was able to move and functionally use my right leg again. He told me that I was a rehab miracle. The truth is, the miracle was God's divine intervention transferred through Patrick's passion for healing, professional skills, and caring personality for his clients, including me. He became not only my therapist but my friend during those sessions."

Patrick was also a devoted son and brother. And he was loved by 22 nieces and nephews and numerous extended family members. He was a good friend to many, but was also humble and felt he only had one friend. His funeral service was standing-room only. He was a great provider for his family, and he worked overtime most weekends to ensure that he could pay for his daughters to go to college. He was unselfish and spent very little money on himself.

I could go on and on, but I think by now, you might be realizing how many people were affected by his death. In my opinion, you have been given the gift of a second chance. Will you choose to continue the same path and risk making a poor choice again? My challenge to you is that you learn from this tragedy. Do your time and then change your life. Do something positive.

Make a difference in the world. Share your story as a lesson to others. I am not ready to offer forgiveness. But, if you want to atone for this, then make your life matter.

I also read aloud the Instagram posts Sierra and Camille wrote on April 20, 2016. At their request, I am not sharing them here.

Dina's Statement

I'm Dina teNyenhuis, Patrick is my brother.

I'm not going to talk about Patrick being senselessly taken away from us because there are no words to describe the grief and anguish, and pain it has caused our family. I'm going to talk about "accidents." What is an accident? I think everyone in this room knows what one is. The problem with accidents is sometimes the Choices We Make are what cause them to happen.

When my students would make poor choices and then claim that the result of their choices "was an accident," I used this example to explain to them that they can't hide behind that excuse: If you choose to climb up on a table and start dancing, then you fall off the table and break your arm, or another student's arm—it was your choice to climb on the table—something you shouldn't have done in the first place, that led to the "accident," even if you didn't intend to fall off.

If we make choices to do certain things or choose a certain type of lifestyle, there are consequences to those choices and to the "accidents" those choices lead to. We put ourselves in positions that can cause negative circumstances or "accidents." Those are within our control. Our negative choices caused them.

December 22, 2017
Denny's Letter

The Honorable Ralph Nunez Fresno County Superior Court Judge Nunez,

We understand that today you will decide whether the defendant has successfully completed his sentence of a court-ordered drug diversion program in the case that stemmed from the death of Patrick John teNyenhuis.

As a family, we have mixed feelings about the news that the defendant may be released.

Justice for Patrick has been hard to find in this case, not through any errors of the court, but for the simple and terrible truth that, as a society, we don't have an adequate punishment when the selfish act of one person costs another his life.

This was not an accidental death. The defendant made a series of choices and committed a series of deliberate acts that ended Patrick's life. No punishment for the defendant can change what he has done or give us back what he took from us.

Our best hope is that if the defendant is released from his treatment today, he never harms another family as he harmed ours.

With that hope in mind, we ask that you read him this letter and this plea from us.

"You have been given something that you took from Patrick, from his wife, from his children, and from his family. You have been given a chance for a better future. A better future for you, a better future for your children, and a better future for anyone else you would harm if you don't change your life. We ask that you take the lessons you have learned and remake yourself. You owe that to us. You owe that to Patrick. You owe that to your children. Don't waste this chance."

Our combined families wish to thank the Fresno County District Attorney, as well as you and the rest of the staff at the Fresno County Superior Court, for your assistance and compassion during this sad time for our families.

Thank you,

The teNyenhuis, Prandini, and Boyles families

REVIEW INQUIRY

Hey, it's Danell here.

I hope you've enjoyed the book, and found it helpful. I have a favor to ask you.

Would you consider giving it a rating wherever you bought the book? Online book stores are more likely to promote a book when they feel good about its content, and reader reviews are a great barometer for a book's quality.

So please go to the website of wherever you bought the book, search for my name and the book title, and leave a review. If able, perhaps consider adding a picture of you holding the book. That increases the likelihood your review will be accepted!

Many thanks in advance,

Danell teNyenhuis Black

WILL YOU SHARE THE LOVE?

Get this book for a friend, associate, or family member!

If you have found this book valuable and know others who would find it useful, consider buying them a copy as a gift. Special bulk discounts are available if you would like your whole team or organization to benefit from reading this. Just contact danellblackcounselor@gmail.com.

WOULD YOU LIKE DANELL TENYENHUIS BLACK TO SPEAK TO YOUR ORGANIZATION?

Book Danell Now!

Danell teNyenhuis Black is available to accept a limited number of speaking/coaching/training engagements each year. To learn how you can bring her message to your organization, email danellblackcounselor@gmail.com or visit https://danellblack.com/.

ABOUT THE AUTHOR

 Danell teNyenhuis Black, a former teacher, spent 22 years in the health insurance industry until she was suddenly widowed. While processing her husband Patrick's passing, Danell rediscovered her love of writing through her blog, *My Life After Patrick*. Danell returned to school, obtaining her master's degree in professional clinical counseling. She is now a licensed professional clinical counselor who specializes in grief and trauma and is certified in eye movement desensitization reprocessing (EMDR). Danell's life experiences uniquely prepared her to help others who are experiencing unexpected loss. Danell lives in Clovis, California, with her new husband, Bruce, and her daughters.

Danell can be reached at: https://danellblack.com/

www.ingramcontent.com/pod-product-compliance
Lightning Source LLC
Chambersburg PA
CBHW030401130626
46549CB00004B/1584